Silas Seymour

Incidents of a Trip through the Great Platte Valley to the Rocky Mountains and Laramie Plains

Second Edition

Silas Seymour

Incidents of a Trip through the Great Platte Valley to the Rocky Mountains and Laramie Plains
Second Edition

ISBN/EAN: 9783337145880

Printed in Europe, USA, Canada, Australia, Japan

Cover: Foto ©Andreas Hilbeck / pixelio.de

More available books at **www.hansebooks.com**

INCIDENTS OF A TRIP

THROUGH THE

GREAT PLATTE VALLEY,

TO THE

ROCKY MOUNTAINS

AND

LARAMIE PLAINS,

IN THE FALL OF 1866,

WITH A SYNOPTICAL STATEMENT OF THE VARIOUS PACIFIC RAILROADS,

AND AN ACCOUNT OF THE GREAT

UNION PACIFIC RAILROAD EXCURSION

TO THE ONE HUNDREDTH MERIDIAN OF LONGITUDE.

SECOND EDITION.

New York:

D. VAN NOSTRAND, No. 192 BROADWAY.

1867.

TO MAJOR-GENERAL JOHN A. DIX,

President of the Union Pacific Railroad Company ;
American Minister to the Court of France, etc.

GENERAL : The following narrative of personal inci-
dents, connected with a professional visit to the Rocky
Mountains, and Laramie Plains, during the months of
September, October and November of the past year, in
company with Hon. Jesse L. Williams, Government
Director, and Gen. G. M. Dodge, Chief Engineer of the
Union Pacific Railroad, was originally written for, and
all but the last three numbers, published in the " New
York Times."

Your appointment by the President of the United
States, as Foreign Minister, made it necessary for you to
leave the country before the numbers were all published ;
and also prevented you, much to the disappointment of
yourself as well as of your associates in the management
of the road, from participating in the great celebration
of the completion of the Union Pacific Railroad to the
one hundredth meridian of longitude, which is imper-
fectly described in the last numbers.

I have, therefore, taken the liberty of collecting,
revising, and dedicating them to you, in their present

form, hoping that their perusal may afford you some pleasure in your moments of relaxation from the cares and responsibilities connected with your high official position.

I have the honor to be, General,

Your obedient servant,

SILAS SEYMOUR.

NEW YORK, *Feb.* 1, 1867.

CONTENTS.

WESTERN INCIDENTS.

I.

NEW YORK TO PITTSBURGH, CHICAGO, OMAHA, FORT KEARNY, AND DENVER—TRIP OVER THE UNION PACIFIC RAILROAD—VISIT OF GOVERNMENT DIRECTORS—FIRST VIEW OF THE ROCKY MOUNTAINS—DENVER CITY.

DENVER CITY, COLORADO, *Monday, Sept. 17, 1866.*

IT is now about two weeks since I left New York, in company with the Government Directors of the Union Pacific Railroad, for the purpose of inspecting the rapid construction of that greatest of modern enterprises; and also examining the different routes which have been proposed for the road through the passes of the Rocky Mountains; and it seems to me that during that time I have learned more of the vast extent and resources of our continent than I had ever known before.

Leaving New York on the evening of the 4th September, by the New Jersey, and Pennsylvania Central Railroads, we arrived at Pittsburgh on the 5th for dinner, after which we were placed in the Government Presidential car, which conveyed us most comfortably to Chicago in time to witness the interesting ceremonies of laying the corner-stone of the Douglas monument, pay our respects to the Presidential party, and hear the eloquent address of General Dix.

On Friday evening, the 7th, we continued our journey from Chicago westward over the Iowa division of the

Chicago and Northwestern Railroad, in the magnificent Directors' car, which was kindly placed at the disposal of the Government Directors by Mr. Dunlap, the General Superintendent, and which conveyed us to the end of the track, a distance of about four hundred miles west of Chicago. From this point we were compelled to make the balance of the distance to Omaha, about ninety miles, by stage. The rails are to be laid, however, upon this portion of the route by the 1st of April next.

We arrived at Omaha, the eastern terminus of the Union Pacific Railroad, on the morning of the 10th, and spent the day in examining the extensive shops of the Company, which have all been constructed within the past year.

TRIP OVER THE UNION PACIFIC RAILROAD.

On the morning of the 11th, the Directors accompanied by Gen. G. M. Dodge, Chief Engineer, Major Bent, Major Chesbrough and myself, took a special train, in charge of Mr. S. B. Reed, the General Superintendent, for the end of the track, which was then laid two hundred and seventeen miles westward, in the Great Platte Valley. We arrived opposite Fort Kearny at four P. M., having passed over two hundred miles of road in eight hours, or at the rate of twenty-five miles an hour.

It may not be improper to state in this connection, that only forty miles of track were laid on this road during the latter part of 1865. And the balance, or about one hundred and eighty miles, has been laid during the present season ; and the track-laying is now progressing so rapidly that it will reach the crossing of the North Platte river, a distance of two hundred and eighty-five miles from Omaha, by the 1st of November.

VISIT OF GOVERNMENT DIRECTORS.

The law requires the President of the United States to appoint five Directors to represent the Government in the management of the road. And it also requires these Directors to visit the road as often as they think proper, and make a report upon its condition, management, and progress, to the Secretary of the Interior.

The following are the names of these Directors—Hon. George Ashmun, of Mass.; Hon. Jesse L. Williams, of Ind.; Hon. T. J. Carter, of Ill.; Hon. Springer Harbaugh, of Penn.; and Hon. Charles T. Sherman, of Ohio. Mr. Ashmun did not accompany the party.

Our party separated at Kearny Station, and three of the Government Directors, Messrs. Harbaugh, Carter, and Sherman, remained on the north side of the Platte for the purpose of inspecting the balance of the completed portion of the road, and then returning eastward. While the other Government Director, Hon. Jesse L. Williams, who is also an engineer of great experience, together with Gen. G. M. Dodge, Major Chesbrough and myself, crossed over to the stage station, near Fort Kearny, for the purpose of continuing our journey by stage to the Rocky Mountains.

FROM FORT KEARNY TO DENVER CITY.

We left Fort Kearny at one P. M., on Wednesday, the 12th inst., and arrived at Denver at ten A. M., on the following Saturday, making the entire distance of four hundred miles in less than three days and nights. The speed, comfort, and regularity of these Ben Holladay Overland stages is certainly astonishing, when we con-

sider the fact that they pass through hundreds and thousands of miles of almost uninhabited country; and that it
is only five years since the experiment was first attempted.
Our party was exceedingly fortunate in falling in company
with Gen. Hughes, the attorney of the Stage Company,
who, with his daughter, accompanied us from Omaha to
Denver.

FIRST VIEW OF THE ROCKY MOUNTAINS.

Our first view of the Rocky Mountains was from a
point on the Plains about one hundred miles distant,
and about an hour before sunset on Friday evening, the
14th inst. A heavy cloud had been lying along the western horizon during the whole afternoon, and it was feared
that we should not obtain the long coveted view before
the following morning; but, fortunately, the sun broke
through and dispelled the lower belt of clouds just in time
to give us a magnificent view of the entire range, and enable us to see the setting of the sun behind Long's Peak,
the highest in the range.

DENVER CITY.

The appearance of Denver, as you approach it from
the east, is not very imposing. The town is situated in
the valley of the South Platte, at the mouth of Cherry
Creek, about twelve miles in a direct line from the base
of the mountains. And the swell, or elevation of the
plain to the eastward, hides it from view until you approach within about three miles of the town. It then
bursts upon the view as if by magic; and presents a
most comfortable and inviting appearance to the weary
traveller from the Plains, who has seen nothing but log

and adobe ranches, at intervals of ten and twenty miles, for many long and weary days and nights.

Denver boasts of four or five thousand inhabitants. The streets are regularly laid out ; and there are many fine brick blocks,·either constructed or in course of construction. You can purchase almost anything here that can be purchased in New York, but at prices from fifty to one hundred per cent. higher. The hotels are very ordinary. Nothing would improve the town more than the construction of two or three first-class hotels.

We are about to start on our trip through the mountains by way of Golden City, Idaho, and Empire City, to Berthoud's Pass.

General Dodge and Major Chesbrough will go from here directly to Laporte, where Mr. Williams and myself are to join them after our return from the mountains.

II.

EMPIRE CITY, COLORADO, *September* 19, 1866.

Hon. Jesse L. Williams, one of the Government Directors of the Union Pacific Railroad, and myself, accompanied on horseback by Mr. P. T. Brown, the Assistant
Engineer, who had been making the surveys for the
road through this wild and forbidding portion of the
route, started out from Denver on the morning of the
17th, in a comfortable covered carriage, drawn by a pair
of lazy, broken down mules, these being considered the
most safe and reliable for the rough mountain roads we
were to traverse. The *outfit*, as all conveyances are
designated in this country, was under the special charge
of Mr. Brooks, a most venerable and experienced moun-
taineer and driver. Our objective point was Berthoud
Pass, and our route lay up the Valley of Clear Creek, or
as near it as the road would allow us to travel.

From Denver, the base of the mountains appears so
near as to invite a short morning walk to them before
breakfast; but we only reached them after a long two
hours' ride of twelve miles, behind our "safe and reliable" mules, over the intervening plains. We entered
the somewhat broken and irregular base of the first
range, or Table Mountain, as it is called, through the
opening made by the Valley of Clear Creek, instead of by

the regularly travelled road some miles further south; and made our first halt at Golden City, fourteen miles from Denver. This place is most beautiful for situation; and should have been the great commercial city for the mining interests of this portion of Colorado. But Denver, during the Cherry Creek excitement years ago, obtained a long distance the start of it, and will, from present appearances, retain the advantage. Here we found iron-ore, coal and fire-clay in abundance, all which will, sooner or later, be turned to good account.

GETTING INTO THE MOUNTAINS.

It being impossible to follow further up the Valley of Clear Creek, on account of the intervening cañon extending some twelve or fifteen miles in our proper direction, we were obliged to make a detour to the south, and enter the next range through a less formidable gorge, up which a very good road had been made in the direction of Idaho and Empire Cities. We stopped an hour for a very good dinner at the Genessee Ranch, where we were overtaken by our very intelligent and eccentric friend Wolfe, whose acquaintance we had made at Denver, and who was wending his way to his mines in the mountains with a load of enormous cabbages, turnips, water, musk and other melons, the products of his large and well-cultivated Ranch on Clear Creek, near Denver. After regaling us for dessert with one of his finest melons, Mr. Wolfe opened to us his plans of a new process for separating the precious metals from the quartz; and also his theory for the extinction of cholera; all which, particularly the melons, it is needless to say, met with our unqualified approbation.

CLEAR CREEK VALLEY.

Our road towards Idaho now lay over a very rough, precipitous country, to a point a few miles below that city, where we again struck the Valley of Clear Creek. As we followed along the abrupt windings of this valley, we were continually reminded of the insatiate thirst of man for the filthy lucre *gold*, by the broken and decaying flumes and water wheels, and the crumbling and half-refilled excavations in the banks along the stream, which had been made and used by the earlier pioneers in their search for hidden treasure. Some two miles below Idaho we passed the extensive and more permanent works, now being erected for the same purpose, by Gen. Beaufort for an Eastern company of capitalists.

A NIGHT AT IDAHO.

At early dusk we found ourselves in front of the Beebe House, in Idaho, acknowledged to be the best hotel in Colorado, with good mountain appetites for an excellent supper which awaited us. Our venerable driver, and part owner of our outfit, was almost exhausted by his continuous wallopings of the mules; and our mules (or rather horses by brevet, since the close of the war), were *hors de combat* from the effects of a long drive over rough roads, and the aforesaid wallopings of the venerable driver. On entering the hotel I was most agreeably surprised to find that it was owned and kept by old and familiar friends from Sullivan county, New York; which fact rendered our short stay exceedingly pleasant. The hot springs, ample bathing, and hotel accommodations, render this place the Saratoga of the mountains for the good people of Denver and adjacent cities.

ARRIVAL AT EMPIRE CITY.

An early breakfast enabled us to reach Empire City, eleven miles further up the valley, at eleven o'clock in the morning. At no point along our road were we out of view of the gulch and mountain mining operations, being carried on by the sturdy and adventurous mountaineers.

Mr. Brown had informed us that we could not travel with our carriage nearer than a point about two miles from the pass; and that it would therefore be necessary for Mr. Williams and myself to procure saddlehorses at Empire for the balance of our journey. This, together with our hasty lunch, detained us about an hour at Empire City. In the meantime we were informed by gentlemen at Empire, that we could not make the ascent to the pass and return during the afternoon, and had, therefore, better defer the trip till morning. Mr. Williams, however, was too anxious to take a glimpse of the Pacific slope of the continent, and had come too far for that purpose, to be deterred by any such prognostications; and we therefore set out at twelve on horseback, after arranging with our driver to meet us at five o'clock with the carriage, at the foot of the trail.

Our road, still following the Valley of Clear Creek, was quite good for six miles of the distance, to the foot of the trail which leads from the wagon road up the southerly slope of the valley of a small tributary of Clear Creek, which heads near Berthoud Pass.

We made our way slowly up the trail without much difficulty, although in many places the path was quite steep and sideling, reminding one of the ascent as made years ago from the Glen House to Mount Washington. We dismounted several times to relieve our horses and perhaps for greater safety. When near the top we started up a bevy of mountain grouse, one of which had the audacity to sit out the discharge of our revolvers, upon a limb within twenty feet of us, without evincing greater emotion than an occasional wink of the left eye; but after our pistols were unloaded, Mr. Brown fired a stone at the bird, which struck a tree near by, and caused it to beat a hasty retreat. I had unfortunately left my rifle and fowling-piece in the carriage.

BERTHOUD PASS.

We reached Berthoud Pass at two P. M. on Tuesday, September 18; and were, for the first time in our lives, greeted with a most extended and magnificent view of the Pacific slope of the Western Continent. The summit of the Pass is but a few hundred feet below the timber, or arborescent line; and is about 6,100 feet above Denver City, and 11,200 feet above the level of the sea. The main range, or divide of the continent, was visible to the north and west for a distance of 100 miles at least, far beyond Long's Peak, which reared its bald head, spotted with eternal snow, high above the average level of the range. After spending an hour upon the Pass, and taking such note of the topography as would refresh our memories hereafter, we ascended the point of mountain south of the Pass to an elevation several hundred feet above the tree line, from which the view of Middle Park, the valley of a tributary of Grand River, leading westward from the Pass; and the extended westerly slopes of the Rocky Mountain ranges, formed a most enchanting picture. The exhilarating effects of the high mountain air and sublime scenery, inspired Mr. Williams with a desire for a patriotic song. After some urging from Mr.

Brown and myself, he led off with "Sherman's March to the Sea." Mr. Brown followed with the "Star Spangled Banner," and I closed the exercises with Moore's serenade "Come o'er the Sea," etc., after the style of Major Scholefield, of the "North Woods Walton Club." The entire range, from Long's to Pike's Peak, seemed to catch the inspiration, and join in the chorus.

After concluding that no improvised glee club had ever performed before a more select and appreciative audience; and after refreshing ourselves, and cooling our over-taxed throats with some coarsely granulated snow, at least a century old, which lay at our feet, we commenced the descent at four in the afternoon.

By permission of Mr. Williams, I take pleasure in annexing the following letter written by him from the summit of Berthoud Pass :—

BERTHOUD PASS, ROCKY MOUNTAINS, }
September 18, 1866. }

Editor Fort Wayne Gazette :—

Having reached the summit of this grand mountain range, in company with Col. Seymour, the Consulting Engineer of the Union Pacific Railroad, and Mr. Brown, Assistant Engineer, my first impulse is to write to my friends at home.

One of the experimental surveys for the Union Pacific Railroad follows Clear Creek to this Pass. That valley was therefore our route from Denver, fifty miles east, bringing us through a rich gold mining district. Eight miles back we took saddle-horses, rising by a mule trail sixteen hundred feet in the last one and a half miles. The point on which I write is some six hundred feet above the Pass, about six thousand seven hundred feet above Denver, and about twelve thousand feet above the sea. It appears to be some two or three hundred feet above the line of arborescence, or "tree line," above which no timber or vegetation grows. Patches of last winter's snow are lying around us on northern slopes, and some of them two hundred feet below. The proposed railroad tunnel pierces the mountain far beneath us. From the summit the waters flow to the Pacific through the Colorado of the West, and to the Atlantic through the Platte.

Peaks, five hundred, and one thousand feet higher than this, are near us, while Long's Peak, supposed to be nearly fifteen thousand feet above the sea, is in full view forty miles to the northeast. During the next two weeks, Col. Seymour and myself expect, in company with Gen. Dodge, the Chief Engineer, to look over the routes surveyed across the Black Hill range, one hundred miles north of this place.

The Union Pacific Railroad is under rapid progress. In November next the locomotive is expected to cross the bridge over the North Platte, two hundred and eighty-five miles from Omaha. The opening of this work across the plains, will soon make the people of the States more familiar with this Rocky Mountain range and its grand scenery; and, what is more important, will afford ready access to a new field of enterprise in the work of developing its vast mineral wealth.

J. L. WILLIAMS.

We found our venerable driver at the foot of the trail, as per arrangement; but in order to insure his return to Empire the same night, he had taken the precaution to exchange his mules temporarily, with the Empire land-lord, for a pair of good horses. Mr. Brown and myself kept our saddles till we reached Empire City, at six P. M.; but Mr. Williams, participating to some extent in the peculiar characteristics of a locomotive, from his long ride upon the back of old "Knock-um-Stiff," as he face-tiously styled his horse, concluded to take his accustomed seat in the carriage. On our way down to Empire City, a conspiracy was organized by our venerable driver to make a permanent exchange of his mules with the Empire landlord for his horses, but I am sorry to say that the scheme was not successful.

The name of Bayard Taylor, that greatest of descrip-tive travellers, who had preceded us but a few months over Berthoud Pass, was still fresh in the recollection of the mountain residents who had been favored with his acquaintance.

III.

DENVER CITY, COLORADO, *Thursday, Sept.* 20, 1866.

ON the morning of September 19th, we awakened at
Empire City to find that we were in the midst of a
Rocky Mountain snow-storm. The weather for several
days previous had been delightful—even on the day
before, during our visit to Berthoud Pass, not a cloud
had bedimmed the sky until after sunset, when thin, hazy
clouds began to settle below the mountain tops around
us, all which, we were told, foreboded a storm.

As our venerable driver had not succeeded in his
attempt to impose his old mules upon our worthy host of
the Empire House, in exchange for a pair of horses, we
were compelled to address ourselves to our return journey behind these much-abused animals ; and he to resume
his powerful persuasives of the previous two days. The
snow had not accumulated to any great extent upon the
roads ; but it was falling fast, and prudence enjoined us
to be early on our way. Our hitherto guide, and most
intelligent and agreeable travelling companion, Mr.
Brown, remained at Empire, for the purpose, when the
storm abated, of rejoining his surveying party in the
neighborhood of Boulder Pass.

RETURN FROM EMPIRE.

Starting out at eight, we reached Idaho at ten in the morning, and stopped a few minutes to say some parting words to our friends of the Beebe House. We then commenced the ascent of the Virginia Cañon, and the descent of Russell Gulch, a distance of seven miles to Central City, which we reached at twelve.

I should not omit to mention, that in driving from Idaho to Empire the previous morning, we had met Messrs. Gukin and Ford, artists from Chicago, who were engaged in taking some mountain views; and were on their return from the Parks, where they had been spending the summer months. At their invitation we had promised to call at their camp as we returned, and look over their pictures; but the morning was so stormy, and their quarters looked so uninviting, that we contented ourselves with a passing salute, and a promise to visit their studios in Chicago on some future occasion. The place where we met these gentlemen is but a few miles from the Chicago Lakes, the scene of Bierstadt's great painting of the "Storm in the Rocky Mountains."

The snow had fallen to a depth of from six to eight inches on our arrival at Central City; and we were fully conscious of having lost, by reason of the thick-falling snow, as we passed down Russell Gulch to Central City, many fine views, as well as a passing inspection of some of the finest and most extensive quartz mining and crushing operations now being carried on in this part of the Territory. The result, however, was unavoidable, and we were obliged to content ourselves with such information as our venerable driver could give us, he being familiar with the country, and part owner of some of the mines around us, as well as of the outfit in which we were travelling.

CENTRAL CITY.

Central City seems to be situated at the confluence of several gulches, which, united, form the north branch of Clear Creek; and the streets are made to follow the windings of the beds of the streams. The houses are generally built upon benches cut in the side hill for the different stories, with basements upon the streets; so that, in order to reach the cellar or back-yard, you are frequently compelled to ascend one or two pairs of stairs from the office or dining-room of your hotel. I mention this fact, not so much the result of my own observation, as from information derived from my esteemed friend and travelling companion, Mr. Williams, who spent at least a half hour in an investigation of the subject, immediately upon our arrival at the hotel. Central City boasts of several thousand inhabitants, or, at least, as many as Denver. We noticed several fine blocks of brick and granite buildings, two or three large banking houses, and also the " Big Barn," situated directly in the centre of the city, and which seems to be the general corral for all the town and surrounding country.

After partaking of a very good dinner, and giving such attention to our surroundings as the gloomy state of the weather would permit, we held a consultation as to our future movements. It had been our intention, on leaving Denver, to spend the present afternoon and night here, which would give us an opportunity to examine many of the mines, as well as quartz mills in the vicinity. Mr. Chaffee, Senator-elect from this forthcoming State, whom we had met in Denver, had very kindly promised to meet us here and show us about ; but the violent storm had evidently prevented his coming.

It had also been our desire and intention to spend the one or two following days in an examination of the Boulder Valley and Pass, under the guidance of Mr. Rawlins, whose works are situated on the Boulder ; and whom we had met in Denver ; but he was nowhere to be found. The storm was still raging and the weather growing colder. Icicles a foot in length were hanging from the eaves of the houses. Our venerable driver and more venerable mules also became objects of our deepest solicitude—the driver claiming that the *outfit* was *unfit* to go further this stormy day ; but if we would let him and the mules rest till to-morrow morning, he would then drive us to Denver (forty miles), or perish in the attempt.

We finally concluded that, as the main object of our journey had been accomplished ; and as the state of the weather rendered a further examination of mountain passes and scenery exceedingly unpropitious at the present time, we would turn our faces toward Denver, with a view of reaching there on the following night. To insure this result, it appeared important that we should accomplish a portion of the distance during the present afternoon. We therefore set out again in the storm at four P. M., with the intention of reaching the Junction Ranch, nine miles distant, before nightfall.

BLACK-HAWK AND LYONS MILLS.

On our way down the valley of North Clear Creek, we passed through the town of Black-Hawk, about two miles below Central City, where we stopped an hour to examine two of the largest quartz mills now in operation in this valley. One, the Black-Hawk mill, which adheres to the old method of stamping and washing the ores from the quartz; and the other, the Lyons mill, in which the new process of decomposing the quartz and separating the ores by the action of heat, is being carried on.

This matter of separating the precious metals from the quartz, is one of vast importance to the mining interests of Colorado; and he who shall first succeed in economically and successfully accomplishing the object, will be entitled to the lasting gratitude of "all the world and the rest of mankind." The exact and proper process seems yet to be hidden in the womb of the future; and many an alchemist is now racking his brain, and experimenting in his crucible over his midnight lamp, in the hope of first discovering this great secret in chemical science, which the Almighty has, for some great and wise purpose, thus far withheld from us.

JUNCTION, OR BOUTWELL'S RANCH.

Our journey up the long hill of four or five miles, between the valley of Clear Creek and Junction, was most tedious and uncomfortable. Like most other obstacles in this world, however, it was finally surmounted; and on descending one or two miles beyond the summit, we found ourselves in front of a most excellent and hospitable Ranch, kept by Mr. Boutwell, with a huge fire blazing from a large, old-fashioned fire-place, inviting us to comfort and repose.

A hearty supper, good night's rest, and early breakfast, enabled us on the following morning to resume our journey with every prospect of reaching Denver before night. The storm had passed over, and the weather was clear and cold—snow one foot deep, ice one inch thick, and the thermometer sixteen degrees above zero. Our venerable driver was also in high spirits at the prospect of a speedy termination of his arduous labors. He had frequently bemoaned his fate in having, at his age, and for the first time in his life, become reduced to the level of a common mule driver. The near sorrel mule, whose thick and unfeeling hide had, for three long days, been the recipient of unceasing wallopings from the driver's almost worn-out whip and nearly disabled arm, seemed to be inspired with the idea that he was approaching the end of his journey. His long ears, instead of flopping listlessly back upon his neck, suddenly assumed a rigid position a little forward of the perpendicular; and away he went over the almost trackless road, down hills, through caverns, gulches and gorges, at a rate which seemed to hazard the safety of our outfit, to say nothing of our own lives and limbs, till we reached the foot of Guy's Hill, which suddenly stretched its huge and uncouth sides directly athwart our path.

GUY'S HILL.

The road up this formidable hill is located upon the zigzag principle—that is, it switches back and forth in the gorges, and along the rough mountain sides a distance of nearly two miles from the base to the summit. Fearful tales were told us by our driver, of the many accidents and hair-breadth escapes which had occurred here; and we were impressed with the idea that so important a thoroughfare, and one over which so large a traffic between Denver, and the heart of the mining regions about Central City, was necessarily carried on, should have been made to follow the equally direct, and far more gentle and uniform grades of the Valley of Clear Creek. This will, as a matter of economy, if not necessity, be done sooner or later, either by railroad or turnpike.

Having safely reached the high summit of Guy's Hill, our descent through Golden Gate to Golden City, a dis-

tance of sixteen miles from the junction, was speedy and
uninterrupted.

CLEAR CREEK CAÑON—IRON AND COAL.

Mr. Williams was desirous here, if time permitted, of
making some further examination and notes of the coal
and iron deposits; and also of the lower end of the Clear
Creek cañon. Halting therefore, at eleven o'clock, at the
Cheney House, we were speedily furnished with excellent
saddle-horses, through the kindness of Messrs. Loveland
and Fisher, the former of whom accompanied us some
distance up the cañon; and also over a considerable extent of the outcroppings of iron-ore and coal, of which he
is the principal owner. After which, and the partaking
of a very good dinner, in company with the stage passengers from Denver to Central City, we resumed our journey to Denver.

The snow had nearly disappeared from the surface at
the foot of the mountain ranges; and had left in its place
a deep salvy mud, which rendered the roads heavy and
tedious. The near sorrel mule had evidently lost much
of the interest in our progress which he had so satisfactorily manifested in the earlier part of the day; and his
ears (that unfailing indication of a mule's thoughts) were
manifestly tending considerably backward of the perpendicular. Our venerable driver's right arm, however, had
become well rested, and he was able, by its constant use,
to reach Denver by four o'clock in the afternoon.

ENTRANCE INTO DENVER.

It was, however, at this last stage in our eventful journey, and when near its termination, that Mr. Williams'

commendable desire for further information, came near being the innocent cause of a most serious calamity to our venerable driver and outfit. Mr. Williams had intimated that he would like to approach, and enter the city, by another road from that by which we had departed, so that he might obtain a different view of its present extent and future resources. This induced the driver to take a road which, unfortunately, led past his stable, on the way to the Planter's House, where we were to stop.

On passing the stable, the contest between the driver and mules was most spirited and exciting; business in town for the moment seemed to be suspended; and every one was anxiously awaiting the result of the driver's efforts to reach the hotel on the next block. It was in vain that I suggested that we had plenty of time to stop at the stable, and exchange our outfit before proceeding to the hotel—the driver swore that he would drive the d—n mules to the hotel or h-ll, and he did not much care which. And he came near succeeding in both; for, on finally reaching the hotel, and just as our venerable friend had taken the last article of baggage from the carriage, the pesky animals (if they may be dignified by that respectable name) started off suddenly on their own hook for a run-away. The driver was knocked down while closing the carriage door, but fortunately the wheels did not pass over him. And the outfit went sailing and crashing down the street, among the carriages, and herds of mules and cattle, towards the river.

After recovering from a most improper, but uncontrollable fit of laughter, occasioned by the sudden and very unexpected turn things had taken, I assisted our venerable friend to his feet. He was covered with mud, his countenance was pale with rage and fright, and his lips and clenched teeth muttered curses low but deep against the whole family of mules and their *offspring*, now, henceforth and forever.

The mules and carriage, unimpaired, were soon brought back, however, by an intrepid horseman who had stopped them in their mad career; and the last I saw of our outfit, it was going at double-quick toward the stable, the head of the driver surging above and below the top of the carriage, as he administered to the refractory mules such merited punishment as his remaining strength enabled him to do.

Thus ended our trip to Berthoud Pass, and the Snowy Range of the Rocky Mountains.

IV.

FORT JOHN BUFORD, LARAMIE PLAINS, D. T., }
Thursday, September 27, 1866. }

The first Agricultural Fair of Colorado had been
advertised to come off on Thursday, September 20, and
be continued on Friday and Saturday; but the severe
storm of the preceding Wednesday had made the travelling so bad, that the Committee determined to post-
pone the commencement till Friday, and continue the
exhibition till the following Tuesday.

On Friday morning Mr. Williams and myself were
invited to visit the grounds by General Pierce, the Sur-
veyor-General of the Territory, and General Hughes, the
general agent and attorney for Holladay's Overland Stage
and Express Company. We found that the grounds,
which are situated about one and a half miles to the
northeast of Denver City, consisted of forty acres of most
beautiful plain in the form of a parallelogram, inclosed by
a tight wall, composed of concrete, about two feet thick
and eight feet high. Upon one side of the rectangle was
an elliptical track one half mile in length, for the trial of
the speed of horses and mules; and upon the other side
were innumerable stalls for the exhibition of domestic
animals. In the centre was a large covered amphitheatre,
in which were exhibited the products of the soil, and such
articles of trade and commerce as the mechanical skill of

the Territory could produce. The whole affair, both in its inception and execution, would have done credit to any State east of the Missouri River.

The articles which most attracted our attention were the mammoth specimens of vegetables on exhibition. Such cabbages, beets, turnips, tomatoes and potatoes I have seldom seen at any State or county exhibition in New York, and they were all produced by irrigation.

The farmers with whom we conversed informed us, that they much preferred this sure method of raising a crop, to the uncertainty attending all farming operations in the Eastern States where they had resided; the expense was comparatively trifling, and their preparations for irrigation had now become so far advanced, that they felt sure of being able to supply the entire demand hereafter, and at moderate prices.

The knowledge of this fact has changed my whole former theory on this subject. I had supposed that the immense population which is settling in the mountains, would have to be supplied with agricultural products, for all time, from the productive regions of the lower Platte, and the States of Iowa, Illinois and Missouri. But now I see that all these lands, lying along the eastern base of the Rocky Mountains, and susceptible of being irrigated by the mountain streams, whose sources are the eternal snows upon their summits, will sooner or later be made to produce all that will be required for the millions of hardy mountaineers, whose thirst and search for gold and the other precious metals preclude them from devoting their time to agricultural pursuits, even though the climate and soil of the mountain regions should warrant it.

The specimens of jewelry, saddlery, needle-work and other varieties of mechanical skill too numerous to mention, were remarkable for their ingenuity and perfection.

And we came away from the fair grounds, after witnessing one or two trials of speed between a lot of second or third class trotting horses, impressed with the idea that this young and unfledged State was bound soon to take higher rank in the confederacy than some of the "Old Thirteen."

Under the new programme, the trial of the fastest horses, and riding by the ladies, which we would like much to have seen, had been postponed to the following week.

FROM DENVER TO LAPORTE.

On the afternoon of Saturday, September 22, we again left Denver, by Holladay's Overland Stage Line, for the scene of our future explorations in the Black Hills, north and west of Laporte. The light from the stars and waning moon was barely sufficient to reveal the dim outline of the ragged sides and crest of the mountain ranges as we passed within a few miles of their base, and across Clear, Coal, Boulder, St. Vrain, Little and Big Thomson and Cache la Poudre Creeks, that flow from the huge gorges in their sides.

We reached Laporte, a distance of sixty-seven miles by stage road from Denver, at daybreak on Sunday morning, and found most comfortable quarters at the stage-station, kept by Mr. Taylor; and were joined, in the evening, by General G. M. Dodge, Chief Engineer, and Mr. James A. Evans, Division Engineer, of the Union Pacific Railroad.

We were now about to enter in real earnest upon the rough and adventurous features of our excursion. General Dodge commenced our education by intimating in the most gentle manner, that we would be expected to feed, water and clean our saddle-horses during the trip.

Our host of the Ranch also informed us, that he had no sleeping accommodations for us, and that we had better look around for lodgings.

In view of such an emergency, Mr. Williams and myself had fortunately provided ourselves with plenty of buffalo skins, blankets and ponchos. We therefore intimated to the landlord, that one of us would occupy the lounge in the corner of the dining-room, and the other would sleep on the floor by the stove. Upon this the cook, a buxom middle-aged woman, with a sucking child, called out from the kitchen, in not very gentle tones, that that lounge was her bed. Mr. Chamberlain, an enterprising merchant in the vicinity, here came to our relief, and kindly offered us the use of the floor in the back room of his log-store, which we were very glad to accept.

The following day was spent in making preparations for our intended reconnoissance on horseback, of the Black Hills and Laramie Plains. An easy-going black saddle-horse was procured of Mr. Chamberlain, for the use of Mr. Williams. A chestnut cavalry horse, procured by General Dodge from Fort Collins, was allotted to me. He had previously selected a fine roan from the same place for himself. And Mr. Evans adhered to a large black mule which he had been riding for some days previously. He very kindly offered this mule to Mr. Williams, with the quiet remark, however, that he was apt to *buck* once in a while, which meant, as he afterward explained, that he would occasionally stick his head down between his fore legs, kick up behind, and throw his rider over his head. Mr. Williams having had some experience with mules, on our trip to Berthoud Pass, very promptly declined the offer.

Hon. Green Clay Smith, Governor of Montana, breakfasted with us as he was passing through with his suite, by stage, on his way to the scene of his future labors.

FROM LAPORTE OVER THE BLACK HILL RANGE.

On Tuesday morning, September 25, our party, consisting of Mr. Williams, General Dodge, Mr. Evans and myself, started from Laporte, fully mounted and equipped as cavalry, and armed to the teeth with breech-loading carbines dangling from our saddles, and revolvers buckled around our waists, accompanied by a supply wagon, in charge of Mr. McLain, one of Mr. Evans' assistants, in which were our bedding, and such supplies as we would be likely to want on our trip.

Our course lay up the valley of the Cache la Poudre a few miles, and then we turned more northerly and followed up the valley of one of its tributaries, which again led us into the valleys of the Pitchfork, Stonewall, Poisen and Dale Creeks.

To the right of us, toward the Plains, were what time had suffered to remain of the rough, jagged crests of the secondary formations as they had rested from the great upheaval of this portion of the earth's surface, when, during some former age, Old Vulcan had undoubtedly fallen asleep, and allowed the subterranean fires, which he used in forging those immense iron wedges and other machinery with which he keeps the universe in equilibrium, to attain too great a degree of heat.

To the left of us were the higher and more imperishable *debris* of these same formations, flanked in the distance by the snow-clad summits of the primeval rocks, which have for so many centuries withstood the combined attacks of time and the elements. The objects of more immediate interest, however, were the "Stonewall Cañon," with its perpendicular walls of rock several hundred feet in height; and the "Steamboat Butte," which from a distance presents to view all the characteristics of a steamboat, with upper cabin, chimneys, pilot-house, etc., the passer-by pausing unconsciously to hear the bell ring, and the familiar cry of "All aboard," before it shall start away.

Our wagon, having followed the travelled road, which we were compelled in a great measure to avoid, had obtained some distance the start of us; and we did not overtake it until about two P. M. Having been in the saddle at least six consecutive hours, we were very glad to dismount, and, after unsaddling, watering and picketing our horses, and extending ourselves upon the grass in the shade of the wagon, partake of a lunch which our commissary (McLain) had made ready for us; after which a ride of three hours brought us to Virginia Dale, one of the stations of the Overland Stage Company.

A NIGHT AT VIRGINIA DALE.

This is a most beautiful amphitheatre, surrounded by mountains, with Dale Creek running through the centre; and is near the boundary line between Colorado and Dakotah. Gen. Dodge here suggested that all the requisites for a good camping ground were at hand, to wit—wood, water, and plenty of grass for our animals; but while the wagon was coming up, I took the liberty of riding forward to the stage ranch, and received the gratifying intelligence that the proprietor was prepared and willing to afford both man and beast very comfortable accommodations for the night. Mr. Williams at first objected, saying that he had come out expecting and fully prepared to rough it in the mountains, sleep on the ground, &c., and he thought it was about time to try it; but he finally yielded very gracefully; and, after providing for the comfort of our horses, we soon found ourselves seated before a cheerful fire, talking over the peculiarities of the country and incidents of the day.

A most excellent supper of coffee, warm rolls, boiled potatoes and stewed antelope, together with the fatigues of the day, inclined us to seek early repose; but here a new embarrassment awaited us. There was but one spare bed in the ranch, and there were at least three of our party for whom, with proper deference to age and rank, the enjoyment of this luxury would seem quite appropriate; but both Mr. Williams and Gen. Dodge were inexorable; and I, whose romance had nearly oozed out during the day, was obliged to submit to the mortifying necessity of occupying the comfortable bed, while they camped down in their robes and blankets upon the floor, in opposite corners of the same room.

ANTELOPE PASS AND LARAMIE PLAINS.

We were again on our way early the following morning. Having ordered the wagon to halt for lunch at the Willow Springs stage station, we followed up the valley of Dale Creek in the direction of Antelope Pass, which we reached at one P. M. This pass is supposed to be the lowest point in a depression extending several miles longitudinally along the crest of the Black Hill range, and is about 8,000 feet above the sea. From this summit we were greeted with our first view of Laramie Plains, extending as far to the northward as the eye could reach, bounded on the east by the Black Hills; and on the west by the much higher range of the Medicine Bow Mountains, which form the easterly side of the North Park.

This pass was named "Antelope" by Gen. Case (who first explored it for the Union Pacific Railroad Company in 1864), on account of the numerous herds of antelope that he found in its vicinity. We saw several groups, but they were careful to keep beyond the range of our carbines ; and we were therefore obliged to proceed on our journey with only a mountain grouse, and jack rabbit in our haversacks, which I had brought down with my Ballard carbine during our morning ride.

Our descent toward the Laramie Plains, soon brought us to an intersection with the stage road, which we followed to the station at Willow Springs, where we found our attentive commissary prepared to receive us, with an excellent lunch for ourselves, and provender for our animals.

A further ride of six or eight miles, brought us to Fort "John Buford," just at sunset, where we were most hospitably received and entertained by Col. Mizner, the officer in command. In addition to his own quarters, which he placed at our disposal, he caused to be put up another fine wall-tent for the accommodation of the balance of the party ; and our stay thus far of one night in his camp has been both pleasant and refreshing.

V.

A DAY AT FORT JOHN BUFORD,* ON THE LARAMIE PLAINS—MR.
 WILLIAMS' LETTER—EASTWARD BOUND—DEATH OF THE ELK—
 CROSSING OF THE BLACK HILLS AT EVANS' PASS—DESCENT
 TOWARDS THE PLAINS—CAMP ON DALE CREEK—LONE ROCK—
 NARROW ESCAPE OF A HERD OF ELK—CAMP ON LONE TREE—
 BOX-ELDER—DEATH OF THE ANTELOPE—RETURN TO LAPORTE.

LAPORTE, COLORADO, *Monday, October* 1, 1866.

Thursday, the 27th of September, was spent by our
party at and about Fort John Buford, on the Laramie
Plains. Mr. Evans and myself took a leisurely ride in
the afternoon, of some seven or eight miles down the
Laramie River, for the purpose of inspecting one of the
crossings proposed for the Union Pacific Railroad. Mr.
Williams employed himself in posting up his notes,
writing letters, and examining maps and profiles with
General Dodge. And the General himself examined,
with his military eye, in company with Colonel Mizner,
the extensive warehouses, barracks, etc., which were in
process of construction for the better accommodation
and protection of the troops and their supplies.

The following letter was written by Mr. Williams on
the day of our sojourn at the Fort, a copy of which he
has kindly furnished me :—

FORT JOHN BUFORD, DAKOTAH TERRITORY, *September* 27, 1866.
To the Editor of the Fort Wayne Gazette—

My last was from Berthoud Pass, September 18th. The day was
delightful. The next day we encountered a snow storm. Stopping
half way down the eastern slope of the mountain, we found the snow

---

* Name since changed to "Fort Saunders."

on the morning of the 19th eight inches deep—icicles on the eaves two feet long, and the thermometer only sixteen degrees above zero. West of the mountain range, the snow fell to the depth of two feet, compelling Mr. Brown's engineer party to abandon the survey, for the time being, and cross the range for subsistence for the mules, after dividing with them the rations for the men. At Denver there was but a sprinkling of snow. Such are the varied meteorological effects caused by difference of elevation, and the influence of the mountain range, in arresting and precipitating the moisture.

Passing north to the Black Hills; and beginning the ascent of this range at the Cache-la-Poudre, the largest tributary of the South Platte, which takes its rise in the snowy heights of Long's Peak, we followed on horseback to this place, another of the experimental lines run for the Union Pacific Railroad, crossing at Antelope Pass. Our party in this most interesting reconnoissance consisted of Gen. Dodge, Chief Engineer of the U. P. R. R., Col. Silas Seymour, Consulting Engineer, and Mr. Evans, the engineer who made the surveys. Travelling in a northwest direction, we had the snow-capped peaks of the grand snowy range always in view twenty to thirty miles to the left. The highest altitude reached on this survey is 8,050 feet above the sea. The transition from the sedementary rocks forming the slope near the base, to the granite which everywhere composes the central and higher parts of these mountain ranges, is plainly marked. In the secondary formation, and lying geologically next above the granite, is observed near the base of mountains on both slopes, what our geologist decides to be the veritable " old red sand-stone" of Hugh Miller ; which the genius of that distinguished devotee of geological research invested with so much interest in the scientific circles of Europe.

The valley of the Laramie river, in which we have travelled for twenty miles, on the western side of the mountain, is a vast plain without a shrub. It is twenty-five to thirty miles wide. The groves of pine on the Medicine Bow Mountains, forming its western boundary, and on the Black Hills to the east, is a relief to the view.

Fort Buford, from which I write, is a newly established U. S. military Post, now in the course of erection, taking the place of both Forts Halleck and Collins, which are to be abandoned. It is on the Laramie Plains, 125 miles northwest of Denver, on the road to Salt Lake. The name is in honor of the distinguished Cavalry General, who defeated the rebel General Stewart in Virginia, but died soon afterwards. Col. Mizner, of the 18th U. S. Infantry, who hails from Detroit, is in command. His kindness to our party, while resting here for a day, is unbounded.

From this point we expect to return over another experimental survey, crossing the Black Hills further north at Evans' Pass, and thence to Crow Creek and Lodge Pole Creek—branches of the South Platte. In that section the Indians indulge in mule stealing (and sometimes in scalping their owners), having recently taken seventy mules from a transportation train. General Dodge has been furnished by order of the Department Commander, with an escort of twenty soldiers, ten of whom are mounted.

Major-General Dodge, before the war, was a civil engineer on the railroads of Illinois and Iowa, and had explored, extensively, these plains and mountains. Until recently, he was in command of this military department; and by all these opportunities has acquired much knowledge of the topography of this region. His services in the location of the Pacific Railroad will be valuable, as, in the late war, they were eminently distinguished in the high commands which he held in the Union army. But the people of the Council Bluff district, in Iowa, are about to lay violent hands on him, and, without any effort on his part, make him a member of the Fortieth Congress.

J. L. WILLIAMS.

I desire to add my testimony to that of Mr. Williams, in relation to the perseverance and skill which General Dodge has brought to bear in directing the surveys during the past year, through this difficult and mountainous country. And, also, to the intelligence manifested by Mr. Evans, in all the important details of topography connected with the extensive surveys and reconnoissances made by him for the Railroad Company, during the past three years, upon this and other portions of the line.

Captain McCleary, the very accomplished and gentlemanly officer second in command at the Fort, returned in the evening from a hunting excursion on horseback, with his horse and that of his orderly literally laden with wild geese and ducks, which he had slaughtered during the day on the Laramie River, within a few miles of the Fort.

Arrangements were also made with Colonel Mizner by General Dodge, for an escort of twenty infantry, ten of whom were to be mounted; this precaution being deemed prudent, if not absolutely necessary, on account of the late depredations of the Indians in the vicinity of the route by which we proposed to return.

EASTWARD BOUND.

All preparations being perfected, we bade our friends at the Fort adieu, at an early hour on Friday morning, and started on our backward course. The weather was now, and had during the past few days, been perfectly delightful. The sun, perhaps a little too hot during mid-day, had blistered our ears and noses somewhat; but the soft, balmy air of the Plains tended to elevate our spirits; and the hazy, dreamy state of the atmosphere, rendered the dissolving views of the distant mountains truly enchanting. Our road for several miles was the same which we had previously followed to the Fort.

DEATH OF THE ELK.

On reaching a point some six miles from the Fort, in the vicinity of a beautiful lake, we were electrified by the appearance of a very large and beautiful Elk-Stag upon the verge of the lake; and apparently transfixed to the spot by some mysterious and fatal power which he could not control. Several shots were fired almost simultaneously, and after staggering a few rods he fell. When we reached the noble animal, life was extinct.

Modesty, while it will not justify any material departure from truth, always forbids the historian of any great achievement from arrogating to himself peculiar prowess, or writing himself down the hero of the occasion. Suffice it to say, therefore, that Mr. Williams, whose knowledge of the sporting laws will be unquestioned by those who know him, decided that the splendid horns of the elk, the acknowledged trophies in all game cases of this kind, should be appropriated to me, with the understanding that I should take them to New York and present them, with the united compliments of the party, to Dr. Durant, Vice-President and General Manager of the Union Pacific Railroad; and that a sufficient quantity of steaks for the subsistence of our party during the trip, should be gratuitously distributed. All which was satisfactorily done, and the immense horns made fast to our wagon.*

The animal was estimated to weigh at least eight hundred pounds.

EVANS' PASS.

After following the travelled road to a point within about two miles of the Willow Spring Station, we diverged to the left, in a more northerly direction, and ascended the westerly slope of the Black Hills to a depression in their summit, some miles north of Antelope Pass, and considerably to the south of Cheyenne Pass, named Evans' Pass, in honor of the Engineer of that name, who formed one of our party; and to whose energy, and skill in his profession, the Railroad Company are indebted for most of the information in their possession respecting the region over which we were travelling.

---

* These horns have been elegantly mounted, and may now be seen at the office of the Company in New York.

FISHERMEN'S LUCK.

We reached our camping ground, in the beautiful valley of Dale Creek, at four o'clock in the afternoon, having ridden about sixteen miles. Gen. Dodge had promised to regale us with plenty of speckled trout, from the clear, cold mountain streams along our route; but up to this time, the only ones we had seen or tasted were upon the dinner table of our excellent and hospitable friend, Gen. Pierce, of Denver City.

As we were watering our animals in Dale Creek, just previous to our halt for the day, the General declared that he saw several speckled trout in the stream; and immediate preparations were therefore made to secure sufficient for our supper. The General and myself trolled the stream for a half mile in each direction, Mr. Williams following with a gunny-sack in which to bag our prey; but it was of no avail; not a bite, nor even the faintest nibble, did I have; but the General protested to at least one fair bite, and some half-dozen glimpses of the little rascals as they dodged around the bends in the stream. We were therefore compelled to fall back upon our regular bill of fare for dinner, aided by our elk-steaks, which, being fried with bacon, we found most excellent.

CAMPING OUT.

We had at last reached the realization of our hopes and dreams, and were actually "camping out" in the mountains. We could roll in the long grass, drink our fill from the sparkling stream, sing and halloo as loud as we pleased, without disturbing any one outside of our own little party. The Indians might be watching us from some of the surrounding crags, and coveting our scalps as trophies for the adornment of their wigwams; or might be planning an escapade for our stock; but what matter—we all felt that innate sense of security and reliance upon ourselves, which always accompanies a wild and roving mountain life; and which, we felt confident, would enable us to cope successfully with five times our number of these savage denizens of the forest.

Our "headquarters" had been furnished, through the kindness of Col. Mizner, with two wedge tents, each capable of sheltering and sleeping two persons comfortably; these were pitched near our wagon; and the wagons and tents of our escort were distributed at a respectful distance in our rear. The General gave the necessary instructions to the Sergeant in command of the escort, respecting the careful picketing of our stock, and the posting of the guard for the protection of our camp from surprise during the night; and after we had indulged in our most comfortable evening talk and smoke, by the light of our waning camp-fire, we were admonished by the cool evening air, and the noiseless quiet which reigned around us, that it was time for us to retire to rest.

LONE ROCK—ESCAPE OF AN ANTELOPE.

After an early breakfast the following morning, we pursued our way over the high and somewhat broken divides till we reached the plain which stretches itself between the valleys of Lone Tree and Crow Creeks. On passing an immense detached pile of granite rock, eighty feet high, and fifty feet square at the base, Gen. Dodge and Mr. Evans ascended with some difficulty to its summit, and reported a most extended view of the surrounding country.

A little further on, while most of our party were collected upon an eminence, some of the escort started up an antelope at some distance from us, which, from the shouts and firing of its pursuers, became almost frantic with fright; and, after circling partly round the hill, actually approached so near to where we stood that we could distinctly see its wild, staring eyes, and panting chest. Stopping for a moment immediately in front of us, it seemed to take in the situation at a glance, when it turned and left us like the wind. Several shots were fired at the beautiful animal, but it seemed to have a charmed life.

NARROW ESCAPE OF A HERD OF ELK.

Still further on we espied, at a distance of about a quarter of a mile in advance, a herd of some thirty elk, quietly reposing in the valley. Gen. Dodge, Mr. Evans, and myself immediately dismounted, and endeavored to make our way to the shelter of an intervening ledge before they should discover us; but what was our chagrin upon reaching the desired spot, which was within easy range of our carbines, to find that some of the escort, in hurrying over a hill to our right, had alarmed the herd; and that they were flying from us at full speed. These, with an occasional shot at a sage hen, or far-off antelope, comprised the only sporting recreations of the day. We made our camp in the valley of Lone Tree Creek at four P. M., having travelled eighteen miles from our camp of the previous night.

After partaking of our frugal dinner, and arranging matters for the night, Mr. Evans and myself strolled a few miles up the creek, in the faint hope of meeting again with the herd of elk which had fled in this direction; but they were nowhere to be seen.

The next day being Sunday; and, as

"The sound of the church-going bell,
Those valleys and rocks never heard—"

we concluded to work our way out upon the Plains by
easy stages, and camp sufficiently far in advance to enable
us to reach Laporte for dinner on the following day. We
stopped an hour or so in the middle of the day, at Jack's
Springs, where General Dodge regaled us with lunch from
a French patti of plover, which was most excellent, and
should form a staple for all self-subsisting travellers. At
four P. M. we reached the valley of Box-Elder Creek, and
encamped for the night.

Our route during most of the day had passed over the
heavy swells, or sedimentary formations, which lie between the former base of the mountains and the present
level of the plains; and which were formed, undoubtedly, by *débris* of the more perishable rocks, brought
down by the mountain torrents, and deposited in long,
irregular slopes at their base.

DEATH OF THE ANTELOPE.

On Monday morning we resumed our course towards
Laporte, having left our escort to await orders at Camp
Box-Elder. Our route lay over very much the same
character of country as we had traversed the previous
day. When at a distance of about two miles from camp,
Mr. Williams, who was riding in advance, observed an
antelope, lying down, some three or four hundred yards
directly in our front. He quietly halted until the balance
of the party came up, when General Dodge and myself
dismounted and prepared for action; Messrs. Williams
and Evans remaining in their saddles, the better to
observe the effect of our guns.

The General, from his long practice, was able to unlimber his carbine and bring it to bear before I was quite prepared, and consequently obtained the first shot, upon which the animal, evidently aroused from a quiet sleep, quickly arose to its feet, and looked toward us for an explanation.

Seeing my advantage, and having observed that the General's ball struck the ground some distance short of the antelope, I concluded that the distance was too great for a point blank range, and therefore decided to fire upon the *ricochet* principle, which proved entirely successful. The animal fell instantly, and when we reached the spot was almost lifeless from loss of blood, caused by the passage of the ball through the neck, and severing the carotid artery. Mr. Williams, although evidently entertaining some doubts as to the legitimacy of the shot, manifested great delight at the result; and, without intending any disrespect to General Dodge, whose reputation for skill in bagging much larger game had become so well established during the late war, immediately pronounced me the *huntist* of the party, and awarded me the beautiful skin as an additional trophy. Our commissary, McLain, on coming up soon afterward, hung the antelope upon the elk-horns at the rear of the wagon, and thus followed us triumphantly into Laporte, where we arrived at eleven A. M.

END OF THE MOUNTAIN EXCURSION.

Thus ended the equestrian part of our excursion. The exercise had been long and somewhat severe; but the natural as well as professional interest which Mr. Williams and myself had taken in the features of the country (150 miles of which we had traversed on horseback during the past six days), together with, to us, the unusual and exciting incidents connected with mountain camp-life, had made the time pass most pleasantly; and caused us to regret the pressure of other engagements which would soon compel us to leave it, and part, for a time, at least, with our most attentive and agreeable travel-ling companions.

My faithful horse had also become an object of sincere attachment. His fast, ambling gait was most easy and comfortable, after the first one or two days of *back*-clima-tion; and he had never failed me, either in a sudden dash across the plain after an antelope, or the difficult crossing of a mountain-ledge or chasm; and I parted from him with sincere regret.

But I fear it was not so with my friend Mr. Williams, whose black horse "Chug-water" (which name he gave him on account of some peculiarity in his gait) came near failing him on several occasions; once, I recollect, when he stumbled and broke his saddle-girth; and quite fre-quently when he would persistently try to descend a hill *upward*, or, rather I should say, sideways or backward, instead of the straightforward way *downward*.

VI.

OMAHA, NEBRASKA, *Monday, Oct.* 8, 1866.

After a most excellent parting supper from the antelope, killed the previous day, and other fixings which our hostess, Mrs. Taylor, provided in her best style, Mr. Williams and myself parted from our friends, Gen. Dodge and Mr. Evans, at Laporte, on the evening of October 1, and took the stage for Denver; which place we reached for breakfast on the following morning, without accident or adventure. The succeeding day was spent in preparing for our departure eastward.

On Wednesday morning, October 3, we took our seats in one of Ben Holladay's best coaches, in company with Senator Chaffee, of Central City, Colorado bound for a connection with the somewhat more comfortable cars of the Union Pacific Railroad, at the nearest practicable point, which we hoped to be Plum Creek, or some point further west.

The roads were in excellent condition; and nothing worth noting occurred to break the dull monotony of our passage over the dry and sterile plains, covered with low tufts of yellow frost-bitten grass, and the whitened bones or decaying carcasses of innumerable cattle which had fallen out by the way, until we reached

Fort Kearny on the following Saturday morning for breakfast.

MR. WILLIAMS' THEORY.

Mr. Williams, however, did not lose an opportunity of impressing upon our minds, as we met and passed the long emigrant and freight trains, wending their slow and tedious way to and from the more distant West, the truth and practicability of his favorite theories in relation to the formation and ultimate destiny of this portion of the country, which were:

First.—That the Great Platte Valley, extending, as it does, in a direct line eastward, nearly six hundred miles from the base of the Rocky Mountains to the Missouri Valley, was intended as the great thoroughfare for the overland commerce of the world.

Second.—That the Platte River itself was intended, in the first instance, to supply water to the early pioneers and emigrants in their pilgrimages to and from the Rocky Mountains; and subsequently to afford the means for irrigating the immense plains along its borders; and thus render it eventually one of the finest pastoral and agricultural regions upon the continent. And,

Third.—That the perpetual snows upon the mountains were intended to furnish an unfailing supply of water to the mountain streams which flow into the Platte; and thus, during all time, afford the means of irrigation to the extensive table lands along the eastern base of the mountains.

BEN HOLLADAY! AND FRIENDS.

At Fort Kearny we met the veritable Ben. Holladay himself, with his agent, Mr. Street, and travelling companion, Dr. Sayre, of New York city; together with a select party of friends, who had accompanied him the previous day in a special train over the Union Pacific Railroad from Omaha.

Mr. Holladay was on a tour of inspection over his stage route to Denver and Salt Lake City; and he informed us that he should probably visit San Francisco before returning to New York. We examined with some curiosity his fine private four-horse coach, which seemed perfect in all its appointments, having ample stowage and sleeping accommodations for a party of three or four gentlemen, or even ladies.

Mr. Holladay also informed us, that he could not well shorten up this end of the stage route, and make an earlier connection with the cars, which were now running some forty or fifty miles west of Kearny, until the track had reached a point opposite Cottonwood Station, where the Platte river could be crossed without difficulty. This will be done about the first of November; and then the staging to Denver will be reduced to two days instead of three, as it is at present.

KEARNY TO OMAHA BY RAILROAD.

We crossed the Platte, in company with Mr. Holladay's returning friends, and took a special train for Omaha, over the Union Pacific Railroad, at ten A. M. Here we learned that during our absence, the Government Commissioners had been out and accepted thirty-five additional miles of track, making in all, two hundred and forty-miles of road, from the initial point at Omaha.

The scene along the road was both interesting and exciting. Here was a fine passenger station in course of construction; there, a freight or water station was being put up, as if by magic. Now, we were halted upon a sidetrack to allow a train of thirty or forty cars laden with ties, rails, chairs, and spikes for the track, to pass. And then, we would meet a train laden with stone or other material for the foundations or superstructure of a distant bridge. Everything, and everybody seemed full of life and energy ; and all working to the same great end, and being directed by the same master mind.

TRIBUTE TO THOMAS C. DURANT.

No one who knows Mr. Thomas C. Durant, the Vice-President of the Union Pacific Railroad ; and has witnessed his entire devotion to this great enterprise, and the untiring energy which he has brought to bear in overcoming the many difficulties in its rapid construction, while acting as the principal executive officer of the Company, in the absence of the President, Gen. Dix (whose time, during the late war, was principally devoted to his duties in the army), will hesitate to award to him the highest honors, both as a railroad manager and public benefactor.

One year ago, not a mile of road had been accepted by the Government ; only twelve or fifteen miles had been laid west of Omaha ; and it was struggling along at the rate of from one-quarter to a half mile per day. To-day, two hundred and forty miles of track have been accepted by the Government. Some twelve or fifteen miles additional have been completed, and it is steadily progressing at the rate of from one and a half to two miles per day. Fourteen thousand and two hundred feet, or *two and seven-tenths miles*, have been laid in a single day.

One year ago, the foundations were commenced for the machine shops at the eastern terminus of the road. To-day, they are substantially completed, and in full operation, with stalls for twenty locomotives, and machinery for doing the repairs of three hundred miles of road; also car-shops, manufacturing and turning out two cars each day; and the whole giving employment to three hundred and fifty mechanics.

One year ago, there were only three locomotives and twenty platform cars engaged in the transportation of materials. To-day, there are twenty-three locomotives, and two hundred and fifty freight cars employed in the same business—five first-class passenger cars, with the necessary mail and baggage cars, and two magnificent excursion and sleeping cars, prepared for their appropriate use.

One year ago, passengers for Denver, Salt Lake, and San Francisco were obliged to ride the whole distance from the Missouri river in old-fashioned stage-coaches, hacks or mud-wagons. To-day, there are no stages running east of Fort Kearny; and nearly one half the distance to Denver may be travelled in ten hours, and in the most luxurious passenger cars.

One year ago, every pound of freight, owned either by the Government or individuals, had to be transported west of the Missouri, by means of ox or mule teams, at the slow rate of fifteen or twenty miles per day. To-day, cars heavily laden with Government stores and private freight, destined for the western slope of the continent, are attached to the construction trains, and find their way in twenty-four hours to the end of the track, many miles west of the one hundredth meridian.

One year ago, the great Union Pacific Railroad was regarded as a myth, and the men engaged in and controlling it, as a set of stock-jobbing Wall-street speculators. To-day, it is known and felt to be a power and a reality; and Mr. Durant and his associates are believed to be in earnest, and fully capable of carrying out to successful

completion the mammoth work which they have undertaken.

When it is remembered that this great transition has
been accomplished in one short year, in a country desti-
tute of labor, materials, and supplies; and with nothing
but the dangerous and uncertain navigation of the Missouri River to rely upon during the summer months as a
base of operations, it must be admitted that a new era is
dawning, or rather has already been successfully inaugu-
rated, in the history of railroad construction.

ARRIVAL AT OMAHA—TROUBLES AT THE HERNDON.

Arrriving at the Omaha depot in the early evening, we
were met by our genial friend Major Bent, of burnetiz-
ing notoriety, who kindly assisted us to the Herndon
House, and saw that we were comfortably quartered for
the night.

We found, however, that the Herndon, which has long
been regarded as one of the most prominent institutions
of Omaha, was in a sort of transition state, and its guests,
as the farmers say, "between hay and grass." Our long
time friend, and distinguished host, Mr. Allan, had been
called upon by Dr. Monell, the landlord, to surrender its
use and occupation into the fair hands of Mrs. Brownson, who had recently leased it, and stood ready to enter
upon the duties of hostess as soon as Mr. Allan could
find it convenient to evacuate the premises, all of which
the said Allan seemed in no haste to do.

An entire week had been spent by the parties in strat-
egy and legal skirmishing, during which it was not unusual for Allan, on visiting the kitchen in the morning, to
find Mrs. Brownson's cooking-stove standing in the place
of his own, which had been thrown over the adjoining

fence during the night; and not unfrequently were the
guests of the house stopped in the middle of a meal
(while waiting, perhaps, for more warm cakes), by intelligence from the waiter that the stove had just been thrown
out of the kitchen. Fortunately for us, however, Mrs.
Brownson's stove was outside of the fence when we
arrived, and remained so during the following day,
Sunday.

DEPARTURE OF MR. WILLIAMS.

But the condition of affairs about the hotel seemed
so unsettled and critical that Mr. Williams concluded
to cross over the river to Council Bluffs, during Sunday
afternoon, where he could enjoy that rest and quiet
which he so much needed after his long and fatiguing
journey; and at the same time be prepared to take the
stage on Monday morning for Dennison, and there take
the cars of the Chicago and Northwestern Railroad, for
his home at Fort Wayne, Indiana.

In parting from Mr. Williams, I desire to say, that it
has never been my good fortune to spend so many weeks,
either socially or professionally, with a more agreeable
and intelligent gentleman and travelling companion; and
I hope he may live long to give the world the benefits
of his sound judgment, and professional skill and experience, in all matters connected with our great national
improvements, such as the Union Pacific Railroad, with
which he has been so long, and so honorably connected.

VII.

TWO WEEKS AT OMAHA—WILD GEESE AND DUCK SHOOTING—ADVENT
OF CHICAGO AND NORTHWESTERN RAILROAD AGENTS ON THEIR
WAY TO DENVER—PARTING SPEECH OF MR. TAPPEN—ANTICI-
PATED ARRIVAL OF THE GREAT PACIFIC RAILROAD EXCURSION—
ITS ANTECEDENTS AND OBJECTS—DEPARTURE FROM NEW YORK —
ARRIVAL AT CHICAGO, ST. JOSEPH, AND OMAHA—FORMATION OF
THE ELKHORN CLUB—RECEPTION AND BALL AT OMAHA.

OMAHA, NEBRASKA, *Oct.* 23, 1866.

The difficulties at the Herndon House, heretofore
alluded to, were amicably arranged on the Monday following our arrival from the Rocky Mountains; and Mrs.
Brownson, the new lessee, was fully installed in quiet
possession.

A favored few of the guests were allowed to retain our
rooms in the gloomy, half-deserted house; and vegetate,
as best we could, among the restaurants, until the hotel
could be renovated and refurnished.

Mrs. Brownson will not only prove herself to be a public
benefactor, but do much towards establishing the doctrine
of the social and business equality, and vested rights, of
women, if she succeeds in the hazardous undertaking of
keeping a good hotel. She certainly has the best wishes
of her numerous friends in the town, as well as of the
railroad people and travelling public generally.

But the city of Omaha should boast of several first-
class hotels. The town is growing, and will continue to
grow rapidly. It has the eastern terminus of the Union
Pacific Railroad; and is the half-way point between
Chicago and the Rocky Mountains. No finer site was

ever selected for a large city; and the country about it cannot be excelled for beauty, as well as productiveness. Elegant residences, and large brick blocks of stores, are continually being erected. "The Credit Foncier of America," and other capitalists, are making large investments there, and the inhabitants are wealthy, energetic, and liberal. Why, then, not give us one or two more hotels, equal at least to the Tremont, and Sherman House of Chicago?

WILD GEESE AND DUCK SHOOTING.

Having received orders to remain for the present at Omaha, I was very glad of an opportunity, when other duties would permit, of accompanying my friend Collins on his hunting expeditions to the Florence lakes, a few miles above Omaha, where fat wild geese and ducks did much abound. And here I must be permitted to say, that a young wild goose, when cooked under the supervision of Mrs. Collins, is the finest eating of the feathered game kind that I ever tasted.

My friend Major Bent would sometimes join us in these excursions, and then we would be sure to return with enough game to supply our restaurant table for one or two days.

CHICAGO AND NORTHWESTERN RAILWAY AGENTS.

Another pleasant incident, in this somewhat dull and monotonous period of my Western sojourn, was the advent of Messrs. Tappen, Patrick and Brown, heads of the freight and passenger departments of that "Great connecting link," the Chicago and Northwestern Railroad, who tarried a few days at Council Bluffs and Omaha, as they were passing on their way to Denver, for the purpose of establishing offices, and making other business arrangements in connection with their road, and its far-reaching Western tributaries.

As they started westward, on the morning of the 17th October, in a special train laden with demijohns, cases, canned meats, fruits and pickles, rolls of buffalo robes and blankets; together with almost any number of breech-loading carbines and revolvers, one would think that they expected to spend at least six months among savage beasts and Indians, before returning to the land of civilization.

PARTING SPEECH OF MR. TAPPEN.

When the train was about starting from the depot at Omaha, Mr. Tappen was loudly called upon by his friends who remained behind, for a few parting words. Upon which he promptly made his appearance upon the rear platform, raised his hat, bowed gracefully to the audience, steadied himself by a firm hold upon the railing, and spoke substantially as follows:

"FELLOW-CITIZENS: But a few short years ago, the spot on which my foot now rests, was part and parcel of a *howling* wilderness"—just here, the sudden starting of the train so disturbed the spot upon which the distinguished speaker's foot was resting, that he came near being thrown overboard; but, on recovering himself instantly, he proceeded with great composure to say:

"During a somewhat short but eventful life, I have held every position, from"—at this point, the train being fairly under way, it became quite difficult to hear distinctly, except the closing sentence, which was as follows:

"I leave the *Great connecting link* in your hands, while I proceed to swing around the"—the remainder of this happy speech was lost ; but the speaker evidently alluded to a curve in advance of the train.

The train soon disappeared, but the telegraph wires kept us continually posted, during the day, as to the progress of the party; and the nature of the despatches was such as to afford the most gratifying evidence of the expansive powers of the air and scenery west of the Missouri River, particularly when a party, like our friends, are borne for the first time with railroad speed along the broader expanse of the great Platte Valley, on their westward course to the Rocky Mountains.

The following specimens have fortunately been preserved :

FREMONT, 10:12 A. M.—"Green leaves grew where my hand now rests. Wild beasts roamed unmolested by the hand of man. More to come."

NORTH BEND, 10:35 A. M.—"The shrill whoop of the savage alone broke the solitude and silence of nature. It was at this epoch of our nation's existence, that two solitary horsemen might have been seen—To be continued."

COLUMBUS, 11:25 A. M.—"Or words to that effect. Conclusion."

ANTICIPATED ARRIVAL OF THE GREAT EXCURSION.

By far the most exciting event of all, however, was the official announcement received on Thursday, October 18 that the great Pacific Railroad Excursion had reached Chicago, on its way westward from New York, and that it might be expected to arrive at Omaha on the following Monday morning.

The worthy Mayor immediately convened the Common Council; and the President of the Board of Trade

called that august body together at once, for the purpose
of conferring upon the subject, and giving a proper reception to the distinguished strangers.

It was finally arranged that the freedom of the city
should be tendered to the excursionists; and that a grand
reception ball and supper should be given them at the
Hernden House, on the evening of their arrival in town.

ANTECEDENTS AND OBJECTS OF THE EXCURSION.

Before speaking further of this great excursion, it may
be well to refer briefly to its objects, as well as to its immediate antecedents.

The public generally, is so ignorant respecting the
identity of the many railroads in this country, which bear
in some form the appellation of *Pacific*, that I will take
the liberty of inserting the following letter written upon
that subject, and published for general information, more
than a year ago, in the *National Intelligencer*, at Washington.

The *status* of many of the roads referred to has undoubtedly become changed somewhat since the letter was
written; but it is believed that it will be found substantially correct for our present purpose :—

UNION PACIFIC RAILROAD.

*Confused Ideas as to its Locality—Nine Different Pacific Railroads—
Location and Present Condition of Each—Government Aid, etc.*

OFFICE OF THE UNION PACIFIC RAILROAD COMPANY,
No. 13 WILLIAM STREET, NEW YORK, *February* 10, 1866. }

To the Editors of the National Intelligencer :—

So much doubt and confusion appears to exist in the minds of the
people, and possibly of some members of Congress, in relation to the

locality, present condition, and future prospects of the Union Pacific Railroad, that, with your permission, I will endeavor to throw some light upon the subject.

There are, at the present time, no less than nine different projects, or organizations, known as Pacific railroads—and, consequently, when allusion is made to either one of these, it is erroneously, and sometimes quite injuriously, applied to the one great trunk line chartered by Congress for the purpose of constructing a railroad through the entire Territories of the United States, and thus connecting the railroads of the extreme Eastern and Western States in one continuous line across the continent.

In speaking of these different organizations, I shall refer to them in their proper geographical order, from the east and south to the west and north; and shall endeavor to confine myself to a simple and concise statement of facts:

1. The Pacific Railroad of Missouri, a State organization, extending from the city of St. Louis to the east line of Kansas, at or near Kansas City, a distance of 283 miles. This road is now completed and in operation.

2. The Union Pacific Railway, Eastern Division, extending from the western terminus of the Missouri Pacific Railroad, at the eastern boundary of Kansas, to an intersection with the Union Pacific Railroad, "at a point on the one-hundredth meridian of longitude west from Greenwich, between the south margin of the Republican River and the north margin of the valley of the Platte River, in the Territory of Nebraska, at a point to be fixed by the President of the United States after actual surveys." The total distance is about 380 miles. This is also a State organization, and was formerly known as the "Leavenworth, Pawnee, and Western Railroad Company of Kansas;" but the Company, in 1863, assumed the name of "Union Pacific Railway, Eastern Division," by which title it has since been recognized. This Company receives the same amount and kind of aid from the General Government as the Union Pacific Railroad, which, to avoid repetition, will be described in connection with that road. The laying of track was commenced in 1863, since which sixty-two miles have been completed, and the road is now open for use to Topeka, the capital of the State.

This Company is also required to "build a railroad from the city of Leavenworth, to unite with the main stem at or near the city of Lawrence; but to aid in the construction of said branch the said Company shall not be entitled to any bonds." This branch will be completed early next season.

3. The Central or Atchison Branch of the Union Pacific Railroad, extending from Atchison, on the Missouri river, in Kansas, to an intersection with the Union Pacific Railway, Eastern Division, in the valley of the Kansas River or Republican Fork. This Company by virtue of an assignment from the Hannibal and St. Joseph Railroad Company, receives the same aid from the Government as the Union Pacific Railroad for the first one hundred miles west of the Missouri River. The grading and mechanical work upon the first section of twenty miles is substantially completed, the iron on hand, and track-laying commenced. The second section of twenty miles is under contract to be completed by the first of May next. There is now a railroad connection from the east, via the Hannibal and St. Joseph, and Platte Country railroads, to a point on the east bank of the Missouri opposite Atchison.

4. The Union Pacific Railroad, extending from the western boundary of the State of Iowa, at Omaha, "to the western boundary of the Territory of Nevada, there to connect with the line of the Central Pacific Railroad Company of California," a distance of about sixteen hundred miles. The capital stock is one hundred million dollars. The organization is entirely the creation of Congress, and being located within the Territories, is not subject to any State or municipal regulations. To aid in its construction the Government grants " every alternate section of public land, designated by odd numbers, to the amount of ten alternate sections per mile, on each side of said railroad on the line thereof, and within the limits of twenty miles on each side of said road, not sold, reserved, or otherwise set aside by the United States, and to which a pre-emption or homestead claim may not have attached at the time the line of said road is definitely fixed." The law further provides that " said company shall designate the general route of said road, as near as may be, and shall file a map of the same in the Department of the Interior, whereupon the Secretary of the Interior shall cause the lands within twenty-five miles of said designated route or routes to be withdrawn from pre-emption, private entry, and sale ; and when any portion of said route shall be finally located, the Secretary of the Interior shall cause the said lands hereinbefore granted to be surveyed and set off as fast as may be necessary for the purposes herein named.

To aid further in the construction of this road, the law provides that as certain portions therein specified are fully completed and equipped, the Secretary of the Treasury shall " issue to said Company bonds of the United States of one thousand dollars each, payable in thirty years after date, bearing six per centum per annum interest (said interest payable semi-annually), which interest may be paid in United States Treasury notes, or any other money or currency which the United States have or shall declare lawful money and a legal tender," as follows : " For three hundred miles of said road, most mountainous and difficult of construction, to wit : One hundred and fifty miles westwardly from the eastern base of the Rocky Mountains, and one hundred and fifty miles eastwardly from the western base of the Sierra Nevada Mountains, said points to be fixed by the President of the United States," forty-eight thousand dollars per mile ; and between the sections last named of one hundred and fifty miles each, thirty-two thousand dollars per mile; and for the entire balance of the road, sixteen thousand dollars per mile. These bonds constitute a second mortgage upon the whole line of the railroad, rolling stock, and fixtures, and " one-half of the compensation for services rendered for the Government shall be required to be applied to the payment of the bonds issued by the Government." The Company is also authorized to " issue their first mortgage bonds to an amount not exceeding the amount of the bonds of the United States, and of even tenor and date, time of maturity, rate and character of interest," with the Government bonds, " and the lien of the United States shall be subordinate to " these first mortgage bonds ; and it is also authorized to issue these bonds " to the extent of one hundred miles in advance of a continuous completed line of construction."

The work of construction has been materially hindered during the past year by the delay of the President of the United States in deciding upon a question of location near the eastern terminus. The laying of track was commenced in July last, and forty miles were completed and examined by the Government commissioners on the 6th instant. Since that time the track has been extended to Fremont, fifty-five miles from Omaha. The grading of the first one hundred and ten miles is now completed, and arrangements are perfected for opening one hundred miles to the public before the 4th of July next. The progress of the work is very much retarded and embarrassed by the want of an easterly railroad connection ; but it is hoped that this will be remedied during the present year.

Large and commodious brick shops, engine and station houses have been constructed by the Company at the Eastern terminus of the road, and these will be repeated as often as may be necessary to operate the road successfully.

The surveys of several routes have been extended as far west as the meridian of Salt Lake City, and of one line to the Humboldt Valley; but the location cannot be regarded as definitely fixed beyond the first two hundred miles.

5. The Sioux City and Pacific Railroad, extending from Sioux City, Iowa, on the Missouri River, to a connection with the main line of the Union Pacific Railroad, " said point of junction to be fixed by the President of the United States, not further west than the one hundredth meridian of longitude aforesaid, and on the same terms and conditions as provided in this act" (approved July 1, 1862) "for the construction of the Union Pacific Railroad." This branch was originally to have been constructed by the Union Pacific Railroad Company; but the act of July 1, 1862, was amended by the act of July 2, 1864, so as to release the Union Pacific Company, and authorize the President of the United States to designate a Company to construct it upon the same terms and conditions as were previously granted to the Union Pacific Company, with an additional grant of "alternate sections of land for ten miles in width on each side of the same *along the whole length* of said branch." The President, on the 24th December, 1864, designated the "Sioux City and Pacific Railroad Company" for this purpose. The map designating the general route of the road was filed in the Department of the Interior, June 27, 1865. Nothing further has been done towards its construction.

6. The Central Pacific Railroad of California, extending " from the Pacific coast, at or near San Francisco or the navigable waters of the Sacramento River, to the eastern boundary of California." This is a State organization, but it receives from the General Government the same aid as the Union Pacific Railroad. It has also been authorized by Congress to extend its road one hundred and fifty miles eastward into Nevada, in case the Union Pacific Railroad is not completed to the State line when it arrives there. This Company has transferred to the Western Pacific Railroad Company the right to construct the road to the Pacific coast, and is now engaged in the construction of the line easterly from Sacramento to the State line, a distance of 164 miles. The laying of the track was commenced in June, 1864, and

56 miles of road have since been completed and accepted by the Government. Seventeen additional miles of grading are now completed, and the balance of the grading is well under way. The line, as established by the Company, intersects the easterly boundary of California in the valley of the Truckee River.

7. The Western Pacific Railroad of California, extending from Sacramento to San Francisco, by way of San José, a distance of one hundred and seventy miles. This is also a State organization, and receives, through an assignment from the Central Pacific Railroad Company, which has received the sanction of Congress, the same aid from the Government as the Union and Central Pacific Companies. The line from San José to San Francisco, a distance of fifty miles, is completed. From San José eastward, twenty miles are about completed, and the iron for the balance of the distance to Sacramento is already purchased and going forward. The grading is entirely out of the way.

8. The Southern Pacific Railroad of California, extending from the bay of San Francisco to the port of San Diego, and thence to the east line of the State of California, a distance of about four hundred and twenty miles. Capital $30,000,000. This is a State organization, and receives no aid from the General Government. Very little, if any, work has been done up to the present time.

9. The Northern Pacific Railroad Company, extending from the head of Lake Superior to Puget Sound, "with a branch via the valley of the Columbia River to a point at or near Portland, in the State of Oregon." Capital stock $100,000,000. This Company was chartered by Congress in 1864. The Company receives from the Government "every alternate section of public land, not mineral, designated by odd numbers, to the amount of twenty alternate sections per mile on each side of said railroad line as said Company may adopt, through the Territories of the United States, and ten alternate sections per mile on each side of said railroad whenever it passes through any State, and whenever on the line thereof the United States have full title, not reserved, sold, granted, or otherwise appropriated, and free from pre-emption or other claims or rights at the time the line of said road is definitely fixed, and a plan thereof filed in the office of the Commissioner of the General Land Office ; and whenever prior to that time any of said sections or parts of sections shall have been granted, sold, reserved, occupied by homestead settlers, or pre-empted or

otherwise disposed of, other lands shall be selected by said Company in lieu thereof, under the direction of the Secretary of the Interior, in alternate sections and designated by odd numbers, not more than ten miles beyond the limits of said alternate sections."

I am not aware that anything further than an organization of the Company has been effected up to the present time.

In addition to the above it may be proper to mention the old organization known as the Southern Pacific Railroad, which was intended to run from Memphis to San Diego, about which very little has been heard for some years.

S. SEYMOUR,

Consulting Engineer, U. P. R. R.

GENERAL SIMPSON'S SPEECH.

The following speech of General Simpson, President of the Board of Government Commissioners (copied from the Chicago *Tribune*), delivered at Chicago, on the return of the excursionists, will also be found to contain much interesting and valuable, as well as later information upon this subject :—

MR. MAYOR, LADIES AND GENTLEMEN :—

The interests of the Pacific Railroad have been ably presented by the gentlemen who have preceded me ; but as there are some points upon which they have not touched, and it may be expected of me, as the President of the Board of Commissioners on the road and its branches east of the Rocky Mountains; and the officer to whom has been intrusted by the President of the United States the charge of the road and its branches, so far as concerns the General Government, to say something in this regard, I trust I shall be pardoned for making the following statement :—

MAGNITUDE OF THE ENTERPRISE.

Preliminary, however, to this, I cannot but generally descant upon the magnitude and importance of this great enterprise. If we take a railroad map of our country, we cannot but be struck with the net of railroads which traverse our domain on the east side of the Missouri River, from Maine to Florida. This bird's-eye view immediately evolves the immense traffic, social comfort, and political homogeneity and harmony which these roads must develop and enforce ; and not only so, it also discloses the wonderful progress which has been made in bringing the different sections of the portion of our country alluded to, in close bonds of affiliation, and therefore of Christian love and sympathy.

But still farther scanning the map of our extended country, we find a most important portion of our domain along the Pacific coast, already filled with a teeming population, and capable, agriculturally, mineralogically, commercially, militarily, politically and socially, of still farther development, so remotely situated, with regard to the portion on the east side of the Missouri River—so isolated by distance and barriers of mountain chains and extended deserts, that it at once suggests the deficiency and the absolute requirements of the extension of our railroad system, so as to bring this portion of our republic into closer and more sympathetic relation with the other ; and thus to bind all portions of our country in one homogeneous organism of political, military, social, commercial and Christian nationality and power.

This is to be effected by the Pacific Railroad and branches ; and because of their infinite importance in this respect, their completion ought to be pushed forward by the people and Government with the greatest possible dispatch.

CONGRESSIONAL ACTION.

The acts of Congress bearing on this important project are chiefly the act of July 1, 1862, the act of July 2, 1864, and the act of July 3, 1866. These acts, as they now stand, authorize the construction of one main line, commencing at Omaha, Nebraska, the initial point fixed agreeably to law by the late President Lincoln, and extending westward in the most direct and practicable line, till it meets the Central Pacific Railroad of California, extending eastward from San Francisco. These two Companies are unrestricted in the extent of the road they shall build, except that they are required to locate and join their respective portions in the most direct and practicable manner.

THE UNION PACIFIC ROAD.

The Union Pacific has been constructed and accepted by the President of the United States, west from Omaha to the two hundred and seventieth mile post, or to a point seventy-seven miles west from Fort Kearny ; and the probabilities are that by the setting in of winter there will be about three hundred and ten miles of the road finished ; which will carry it beyond the Forks of the Platte, and embrace the bridge now near completion over the North Fork. The surveys for this road have extended across the Rocky and Wasatch Mountains to the valley of the Humboldt ; and lines of routes have been found which will not require a grade, at any point, over one hundred and sixteen feet per mile, the maximum grade of the Baltimore and Ohio Railroad, and the limit fixed by law.

THE CENTRAL PACIFIC ROAD.

The Central Pacific of California, on the 6th of the present month, had been graded from Sacramento eastwardly to Cisco, a distance of ninety-three miles, or to a point within twelve miles of the summit of the Sierra Nevada ; and the track has been laid from Sacramento, eighty miles of that distance, and the cars are running thereon. The surveys show a perfectly feasible route over the Sierra Nevada, with maximum grades within the limits prescribed by the law ; and as they show a very easy line along the valley of the Humboldt, not requiring a grade over fifty-three feet to the mile, the President of the Company, Leland Stanford, Esq., confidently anticipates that they will be able to reach Great Salt Lake during the year 1870.

BRANCH ROADS.

The branch roads west from the Missouri river joining the Union Pacific Railroad, are, commencing at the most northern point and running southwardly, first :—

THE SIOUX CITY AND PACIFIC RAILROAD,

extending from Sioux City westwardly, and to join in the most practicable and direct manner at such part of the Union Pacific Railroad as the Company may select. Surveys, I have been informed by Mr. John J. Blair, the President of this Company, have been made for this road, but as they have not yet been officially reported to the Government, the final location of the route has not yet been established, and nothing further remains to be said than that no work has yet been done on this branch. Next,

THE EXTENSION OF THE BURLINGTON AND MISSOURI RIVER RAILROAD,

which by law is to cross the Missouri River south of the mouth of the Platte, and, according to the map filed in the Interior Department, has been located by the Company as far as Kearny City, along the south side of the Platte, and getting into the Platte Valley again within eighteen or twenty miles east of Fort Kearny. The road is to join the Union Pacific, not further west than the one hundredth meridian of west longitude. No work has been commenced on this branch. Next,

THE EXTENSION OF THE HANNIBAL AND ST. JOSEPH RAILROAD, BY THE WAY OF ATCHISON,

which the Company have, by law, the option of connecting in the most direct and feasible way with the Union Pacific, not farther west than the one hundredth meridian, or the Union Pacific, Eastern Division, without restriction to distance. Twenty miles of this road west from Atchison has been constructed and accepted by the President of the United States, and another section of twenty miles is represented to be nearly ready for examination by the Commissioners. The next branch is

THE UNION PACIFIC RAILWAY, EASTERN DIVISION,

which starts from the mouth of the Kansas River, on its south side, and has been located up the valley of the Kansas River as far as Fort Riley, and thence across to and up the valley of the Smoky Hill Fork, as far as the western boundary of Kansas ; thence it is to go to Denver City, and join the Union Pacific at a point not farther than fifty miles west from the meridian of Denver. This road has been accepted by the President of the United States for a distance of one hundred and thirty miles west from the initial point at the mouth of the Missouri River, and has been represented recently as completed and the cars running thereon as far as Fort Riley, a distance of one hundred and thirty-six miles.

GOVERNMENT AID.

The Union Pacific and the Central Pacific Railroad of California, on the completion of sections of not less than twenty miles of their roads, will be alike entitled to bonds respectively from the Government to the extent of $16,000 per mile from their initial points to the east line of the Rocky Mountains, and to the west base of the Sierra Nevada, thence across the Rocky Mountains to the west base of the same for a distance of one hundred and fifty miles, and across the Sierra Nevada to the east base of the same for a distance of one hundred and fifty miles, they respectively got three times $16,000, or $48,000 per mile. Between the western base of the Rocky Mountains and the eastern base of the. Sierra Nevada, they will be entitled to twice $16,000, or $32,000 per mile.

Both these Companies will, by law, be entitled to ten alternate odd sections of land on each side of their road, not sold, reserved, or otherwise disposed of by the United States, and to which a pre-emption or homestead claim may not have been attached.

The Union Pacific Railway, Eastern Division, (properly the Southern Division), agreeably to the act of July 3, 1866, receives, on the completion of sections of at least twenty miles of its road, $16,000 per mile, for a distance from its initial point at the mouth of the Kansas River, as far westward as would be equal to the length of its road, had it, according to the act of July 1, 1862, joined the Pacific Railroad on the one hundredth meridian of longitude, between the north bank of the Platte River, and the south bank of the Republican Fork of the Kansas River. This road is entitled, in addition, on the completion of sections of not less than twenty miles of its road, to ten alternate odd sections of land on each side of its line, subject to the reservations, as in the case of the Union Pacific and Central Pacific Railroad before stated.

The Atchison and Pike's Peak Railroad, or Pacific extension of the Hannibal and St. Joseph Railroad, on the completion of sections of not less than twenty miles, gets bonds of $16,000 and ten alternate sections of land on each side of the road, per mile, but only for a distance of one hundred miles west from Atchison.

The Sioux City Pacific Railroad under the act of July 2, 1864, is entitled to bonds of $16,000 per mile on the completion of sections of not less than twenty miles, for a distance from the initial point at Sioux City, not greater than it would have been entitled to under the act of July 1, 1862, which restricted its junction with the Union Pacific, at a point not farther west than the one hundredth meridian of west longitude. This road also gets land, but only to the extent of five alternate sections within a limit of ten miles on each side of the road, with the same restrictions as stated in the case of the roads already mentioned.

The Pacific extension of the Burlington and Missouri River Railroad, by the act of July 2, 1864, is not entitled to bonds, but to lands to the extent of ten alternate odd sections on each side of its line of route.

THE COMPLETION OF THE ROADS.

Having thus given the chief points of the law with regard to the Union Pacific Railroad and branches, I would recall your attention to the anticipation confidently entertained by Mr. Stanford, the President of the Central Pacific Company of California, that they will, even under the present law, be able to reach Great Salt Lake during the year 1870. General Dix, the President of the Union Pacific Railroad Company, has informed me that they will meet the Central Pacific, of California in five years ; and, thus, according to both the gentlemen named, we may expect the completion of the road in 1871, or six years before the 1st of July, 1877—the limit fixed by the law. It is submitted, however, that as the work in the Rocky Mountains and Utah will be very heavy, there should be some legislation which will enable the Union Pacific Railway Company to work in advance of their completed line, at least eight hundred miles ; so that the Company could now be employing the Mormons in Utah, who, with the " Gentiles," are willing and anxious to take contracts for grading the road, getting out the ties, and making the necessary iron. The act of July 3, 1866, enables the Union Pacific, and Central Pacific of California, to work three hundred miles in advance of their continuous line ; but while this privilege is probably sufficient for the California Company, on account of the nature of the country through which it will have to construct its road, it is not so for the Union Pacific, whose difficult portions stretch out for so great a distance west of their present work. It is hoped that this matter will receive the attention of Congress at the earliest possible moment.

CONFUSION OF NAMES.

There is another item of legislation required, which has grown out of the confusion that exists with regard to the names of the roads, which should be attended to. The branch road, which starts from the mouth of the Kansas River, is called the Union Pacific Railway, Eastern Division. The consequence is, that though this road is being made by an entirely different Company from the Union Pacific Railroad Company, which is constructing its road all the way through from Omaha, till it meets the Central Pacific of California, the credit or discredit which attaches to the one naturally attaches to the other, to the enhancement or depreciation of its bonds ; and already I am informed there have been considerable serious misapprehensions existing on this account, to the advantage or detriment of one or the other Company. This liability to error can only be obviated by Congress changing the name of the Union Pacific Railway, Eastern Division, so that it may not by any possibility be confounded with the Union Pacific Railroad, with which it is in no way pecuniarily connected. A sufficiently distinctive name would be the Kansas River Branch of the Union Pacific Railroad.

BENEFITS TO CHICAGO.

Thus, Mr. Mayor, ladies and gentlemen, I have at some length given you a description of the Union Pacific Railroad and branches, with the provisions of law relating thereto ; but I cannot close my remarks without pointing out to you the great benefits which must inure to your city from the completion of this great highway of nations. Standing as you do pre-eminently related to the great lakes of the North ; and by your railroads with all portions of the United States on the east side of the Rocky Mountains, with the prestige of your past and present growth ; and immediately on the great airline route across the continent from New York, you cannot but become the great *entre-dépôt* of trade and travel of the world ; and therefore without doubt one of the greatest cities of the world—second on this continent to probably only the metropolis of New York.

Adding my thanks to those of the gentlemen who have preceded me for the very kind and munificent reception which the Union Pacific Railroad excursion party has received at your hands, I will here close my already, I fear, too extended remarks.

The laws of Congress require that the first one hundred miles of the Union Pacific Railroad, west of the Missouri River, shall be completed on or before the 27th June, 1866; and that it shall be completed to the one-hundreth meridian of longitude, a distance of one hundred and forty-seven miles further, at the rate of one hundred miles per year thereafter; or, say, by the middle of December, 1867.

The Railroad Company however, had, in utter disregard of all precedents in railroad construction, completed the first one hundred miles on June 2d, 1866, and had laid the track across the hundredth meridian on the 5th October of the same year.

In fact, the Company had become so regardless of these precedents, and of the slow progress contemplated by Congress, that it had allowed Mr. Reed, the Engineer in charge of construction, to do the grading, construct the bridges, and lay the superstructure, all complete, upon two hundred and forty-five miles of road in one hundred and eighty-two working days; averaging more than one and one-third miles per day.

It was therefore deemed expedient and proper, by the managers of this great national enterprise, that the completion of the first division, extending from the Missouri River, at Omaha, to the one-hundredth meridian of longitude, within considerably less than a year from the time required by law, should not only be suitably advertised to the world, but satisfactorily verified by the proper officers of the Government, and members of Congress.

Invitations were accordingly extended to the President of the United States, and members of his Cabinet; also to all the members of Congress, Foreign Ministers, military and naval commanders, and to the principal railroad men and leading capitalists throughout the country, to join in a grand excursion from New York City to the one-hundredth meridian, in the Great Platte Valley, a distance of about seventeen hundred miles, and more than half way across the continent.

No railroad excursion of similar character and magnitude had ever been projected in this, or any other country; and the parties most interested were, of course, untiring in their efforts to make it a complete success.

The different lines of connecting railroads, steamboats, and stages between New York and Omaha, were at once placed at the disposal of the Company by their liberal and enterprising managers, who seemed to vie with each other in their efforts to aid the Union Pacific Railroad Company in its great and somewhat novel undertaking.

Very much to the regret of the excursionists, as well as the receptionists along the route, General John A. Dix, the President of the Company, was prevented from accompanying the party, by receiving from the President of the United States, the appointment of Minister to France, just previous to its departure from New York. The charge of the excursion therefore devolved upon Mr. Thomas C. Durant, Vice-President, and Messrs. Sherman, Cook, Dillon, Lambard, and Duff, Directors; assisted by Mr. B. F. Bunker, Assistant Secretary of the

Company, Col. N. A. Gestner and Mr. E. Simmonds, from the New York office.

DEPARTURE FROM NEW YORK.

The party, consisting of about one hundred persons, fully supplied with everything that could be improvised or thought of for its comfort and enjoyment, left New York on Monday evening, October 15th, by way of the New Jersey, and Pennsylvania Central Railroads, to Pittsburgh; and the Pittsburgh Fort Wayne and Chicago Railroad to Chicago, where they arrived in high spirits on the following Wednesday evening.

Considerable accessions of invited guests were made to the party on the way to, and at, Chicago. Messrs. Springer Harbaugh, of Pittsburgh, and Jesse L. Williams, of Fort Wayne, Government Directors of the road, accompanied the excursion to Chicago; but, as both these gentlemen had just returned from a somewhat extended inspection of the road, they were very reluctantly excused from proceeding farther with the party.

Several of the excursionists preferred to remain a day or two at Chicago; and then proceed over the Chicago and Northwestern Railroad, in company with the officers of that Road, to Dennison; and from thence to Omaha by stage. But by far the largest portion, accompanied by the Great Western Light Guard Band, started from Chicago on Thursday morning, October 18th, by way of the Chicago Burlington and Quincy, and the Hannibal and Saint Joseph Railroads, and arrived at St. Joseph on the following Friday evening.

Here they were met by Mr. H. M. Hoxie, the General Western Agent of the Union Pacific Railroad, to whose care had been assigned the transportation on the Missouri River, a distance of two hundred and fifty miles, by river, from St. Joseph to Omaha; and also the subsistence of the entire party until its return to Saint Joseph.

Two of the largest class Missouri River packets—the *Denver*, Captain Waddell, and the *Colorado*, Captain Hooper—with an additional band of music on board, were in readiness to receive the party on its arrival at Saint Joseph; and the excursionists soon found themselves, with bands playing and colors flying, steaming up the great Missouri River, which, for many hundred miles of its turbid, snaggy, barry, winding course, forms the western boundary of the Atlantic portion of the United States.

The journey from Saint Joseph to Omaha was accomplished, without serious accident or detention, in less than forty-eight hours; and the party reached the eastern terminus of the Union Pacific Railroad on Monday morning, the 22d of October, having been on the way from New York a little less than one week.

Some idea of the manner in which the excursionists were subsisted under the supervision of *Professor* Hoxie, while passing up the Missouri River, may be formed by a perusal of the following bills of fare on board the steamers:—

COMPLIMENTARY EXCURSION

TO THE

Chief Owners of all Railroads in the United States,

ON BOARD THE SPLENDID

STEAMER COLORADO.

J. D. HOOPER, Com. | *O. M. BROWN, Clerk.*
B. FORD, General Superintendent Packet Line.

BILL OF FARE.

STEAMER COLORADO, October 20, 1866.

SOUP.

Chicken Gumbo.   Oyster.

FISH.

Baked Pike, Oyster Sauce.   Boiled Trout, a-la Normande.

BOILED.

Leg of Mutton, Caper Sauce.   Ham.   Tongue.
Turkey, Oyster Sauce.   Corned Beef and Cabbage.
Chicken, Egg Sauce.   Beef, a-la-mode.

ROAST.

Turkey, Giblet Sauce.   Saddle Mutton.   Lamb, Barbecued.
Quails on Toast.   Spare-Rib of Pork.   Ribs of Beef.
                      Sugar-Cured Ham, Champagne Sauce.

COLD DISHES.

Chicken Salad, Young America style.   Boned Turkey, with Jelly.
Lobster Salad, Boston style.   Leg of Mutton, Boiled.
Fresh Tongue, in Belvue.   Pressed Corned Beef.
Anchovy Salad.   Ham.   Roast Beef.   Buffalo Tongue.

ENTREES.

Rabbit, sautl, a-la-Chasseur.
Small Patties, a-la-Française.
Lamb Chops, a-la-Millionaire.
Chicken Livers, fried in paper.
Calf's Head, stuffed, a-la-Royal.
Fricassee of Chicken, a-la-Rhine.
Escaloped Oysters, Louisiana style.
Fillets of Beef, larded, a-la-Soubise.
Rice Croquettes, garnished with Preserves.
Fried English Cream, flavored with Vanilla.
Calf's Brains, fried in Batter.
Veal Cutlets, breaded, Sauce Tortue.
Baked Pork and Beans, Boston style.
Prairie Chicken, larded Tomato Sauce.

Vel au Vent, aux buitres.
Petis Pates, garnie a-la-Bechamelle.
Croquettes de Volaille.
Boudins, a-la-Richelieu.
Filet de Bœuf, Sauce Medere.
Supreme de Volaille, aux Champignons.
Canards Braise, aux Oliaes.
Fricandeau de Veau, pica aux Epinards.
Pigeons, Braise, a-la-Financiere.
Baked Salmon, with Cream.
Turkey Giblets, a-la-Valenciene.
Antelope Steak, Sherry Wine Sauce.
Maccaroni, with Oparmesseur Cheese.
Fried Oysters.

Tenderloin of Venison, brazed, a-la-Italian.

GAME.

Antelope, larded, Sauce Bigarade.
Bear, brazed, Port Wine Sauce.
Saddle of Venison, Cranberry Sauce.
Mallard Ducks—Teal Ducks, Malaga Wine Sauce.

Grouse, larded, Madeira Sauce
Quails, on Toast.
Wild Turkey.
Rabbit Pot Pie, Boston style.

VEGETABLES.

Oyster Plant.	Carrots.	Onions.	Boiled Potatoes.
Parsnips.	Turnips.	Sour Crout.	Cabbage.
Hominy.	Boiled Rice.	Mashed Potatoes.	

RELISHES.

Tomato Catsup.	Worcestershire Sauce.	Boston Pickles.
Beets. Celery.	Olives.	Cold Slaw.

PASTRIES.

English Plum Pudding, White Sauce.
Jelly Cake.   Vanilla Ice Cream.
Fruit Cake, ornamented.
Pyramid of Macaroons.
Cranberry Tartlets.   Mince Pie.
Almond Macaroons.

Rum Jelly.
Champagne Jelly.
Chocolate Cake.
Princess Pyramid.
Cream Pie.
Cranberry Tartlets.

Pound Cake.
Lady Fingers.
French Kisses.
Old Castle.
Apple Pie.
Swiss Cottage.

DESSERTS.

Oranges. Pecans. Almonds. Raisins.
Gateau Genoise, a-la-Jelée.
Charlotte Russe au Marasquin.
English Walnut.   Apples.   Figs.

Merungues aux Peches.
Bonbon, a-la-Vanilla.
Bavarois Glace, aux Amandes.
Grapes.   Peaches.   Filberts.   Pears.

TEA, COFFEE AND CHOCOLATE.

HOURS FOR MEALS:

Breakfast........ ....7 to 9 | Dinner..... ....1 to 3
Tea............................6 o'clock.

Union Pacific Railroad Excursion—Road open from Omaha to one-hundredth meridian.

DINNER BILL OF FARE.

—◆◆◆—

STEAMER DENVER.

October 28, 1866.

SOUPS.

Purée of Rabbit, a-la-Chantilly.   Rice Soup, a-la-Florentine.

FISH.

Trout, a-la-Victoria.   Pike, a-la-Chevaliere.

ROAST.

Beef.   Mutton.   Pork.   Pig.   Turkey.   Chicken.   Duck·
                    Veal.   Grouse.

BOILED.

Leg of Mutton, Caper Sauce.   Turkey, Oyster Sauce.   Chicken, Supreme Sauce
            Tongue.   Duffield Ham.   Corned Beef and Cabbage.

VEGETABLES OF THE SEASON.

ENTREES.

Chicken, a-la-Montmorenci.   Chartreuse of Vegetables, garnished with
Cushion of Veal, a-la-St. George.   Partridges.
Timbal of Maccaroni, a-la-Mazarine.   Border of Potato Paste, garnished with
Tourte of Ox, Palates a-la-Francaise.   Calves Brains a-la-Bavigotte.
        Croustade of Bread, garnished with Calves Tails a-la-Poulete.

GAME.

Saddle of Elk, a-la-Bellevue.   Teal Ducks, a-la-Royal.   Snipes, a-la-Essler.
            Pheasants, a-la-Monclas.   Goose, a-la-Anglaise.

COLD DISHES.

Boar's Head, with Aspie Jelly.   Italliene Salad.
Gelatine Turkey, with Aspie Jelly.   Salina of Duck, with Aspie Jelly.

RELISHES.

Celery.   Currant Jelly.   Tomato Catsup.   French Mustard.   Horse Radish.
        Walnut Catsup.   Chow-Chow.   Cold Slaw.   Pineapple Cheese.
            Pickles and Olives.   Mushroom Catsup.   Assorted Sauces.

PASTRY AND DESSERT.

PUDDINGS.
Cocoanut, Cream Sauce.

PIES AND TARTS.
Apple. Peach. Damson. Blackberry. Turnover of Apple. Jelly Tarts.

CAKES.
Pound. Lady. Fruit. Sponge.

CREAMS AND JELLIES.
Maraschino Bavarian Cream.
English Cream, with Peaches.
Orange Jelly, a-la-Anglaise.

Celestine Strawberry Cream,
Pineapple Jelly.
Macedoine of Fruits,

DESSERT.
Web Meringue, a-la-Parisiene.
Cream Fouett, a-la-Printanier.
Fruit Meringues.

Nouilles Cake, a-la-Allemande.
Strawberries and Cream.
Cocoanut Candy.

ORNAMENTS.
Horn of Plenty. Pyramid of Sponge Candy. Pyramid of Rock Candy, Gothic style.
Ornamented Fruit Cake, with Nougat Vase.

NUTS AND FRUITS.
Grapes. Oranges. Apples. Pears. Prunes. Figs. Raisins.
Almonds. English Walnuts. Filberts. Brazil.
Peanuts. Pecans. Dates. Pappas.

COFFEE, TEA AND CREAM.

HOURS FOR MEALS:
Breakfast................7 to 9 | Dinner...................1 to 3
Tea............................6 o'clock.

WILLIAM DWYER, Steward.

FORMATION OF THE ELKHORN CLUB.

That portion of the party which had crossed the State of Iowa by land, including Mr. Perry H. Smith, the Vice-President, and Mr. George L. Dunlap, the General Superintendent of the Chicago and Northwestern Railroad, Messrs. Turner, Ayer, Bowen, Crerer, and several others from Chicago, with the most important addition of Professor Kinsley, the justly celebrated *caterist* of Chicago, and a strong detachment of his assistants, having re-joined the party in the morning, were assigned to quarters on the Railroad Company's steamer *Elkhorn*, which lay at the landing immediately across the bows of the steamer *Denver*.

It should here be recorded for the benefit of all future historians, as well as the "rest of mankind," that, on this memorable day, and upon this veritable steamer *Elkhorn*, the famous, and never-to-be-forgotten *Elkhorn Club* was duly organized and established upon a firm, and it is to be hoped an enduring basis.

RECEPTION AND BALL AT OMAHA.

The authorities of Omaha were on the alert at an early hour for the purpose of welcoming and entertaining the distinguished party. Governor Saunders, Secretary Paddock, Mayor Miller, and Vice-President Patrick, of the Board of Trade, soon made their appearance upon the steamers, and welcomed the excursionists in appropriate speeches, tendering them the freedom of the City and Territory; and inviting them to a reception ball at the Hernden in the evening; all which were duly responded to and accepted by Senator Patterson, Government Director Sherman, and others of the party.

Carriages were in waiting, to convey such of the number as desired to leave the boats, either about the town, to the hotels, or to the residences of several of the private families, which had been most liberally thrown open for the occasion.

The excursionists, with their insignia of ribbons and rosettes, were soon to be seen in all parts of the town, and among the extensive workshops of the Railroad Company, evidently delighted, and somewhat astonished to find themselves, after a week's journeying westward from New York, still among people of wealth, refinement, and enterprise.

The ball in the evening, however, was perhaps the greatest surprise. The presence of General Phillip St. George Cooke, commanding the Department, with his staff; Governor Saunders, Chief-Justice Kellogg, Secretary Paddock, Senators Thayer and Tipton, all of Nebraska; together with the city authorities, and the wealthy, enterprising, business and professional men of Omaha, with their families, all conduced to make it an entertainment which would have done credit to any gathering of a similar character in Chicago, Washington, or New York.

The dance, alternating with the promenade, and a judicious sprinkling of excellent and substantial refreshments, occupied the time most pleasantly till the small morning hours, when all separated in the best of spirits, ready for the new and exciting scenes which were to open upon them on the morrow.

Here we will leave them for the present, and be prepared to accompany them many hundred miles farther westward, towards the never-setting Star of Empire.

4*

VIII.

MORNING AFTER THE BALL—THE EXCURSION TRAIN—ALL ON BOARD
—ITS PROGRESS WESTWARD—THE GREAT PLATTE VALLEY—
STATIONS ON THE ROAD—ARRIVAL AT COLUMBUS—CAMPING OUT
ON THE PLAINS—INDIAN WAR-DANCE—MORNING SERENADE—
TOWN OF COLUMBUS—SHAM INDIAN FIGHT—PRESENTS TO THE
INDIANS—CONTRAST BETWEEN CIVILIZED AND SAVAGE LIFE—
TRAIN STILL GOING WESTWARD—WAY-STATIONS ON THE ROAD—
ARRIVAL AT CAMP NO. 2—MILITARY ENCAMPMENT—ANOTHER
NIGHT IN CAMP—MORNING EXERCISES—DEPARTURE OF THE ELK-
HORNS—MORNING NEWSPAPER—LIST OF EXCURSIONISTS—END
OF TRACK FOUND AT LAST—BUFFALO AND ANTELOPE HUNTERS
—DINNER IN CAMP—FIRE-WORKS ON THE PLAINS—THIRD NIGHT
IN CAMP—HOMEWARD BOUND—ONE HUNDREDTH MERIDIAN—
PRAIRIE-DOG CITY—FIRE ON THE PLAINS—RETURN TO OMAHA—
DEPARTURE OF EXCURSIONISTS EASTWARD—ELKHORN CHEERS TO
MR. DURANT—THEIR SAFE ARRIVAL HOME.

OMAHA, NEBRASKA, *Nov.* 5, 1866.

MORNING AFTER THE BALL.

The elegant entertainment given by the citizens of Nebraska and Omaha to the excursionists the previous
evening, did not prevent them from being astir at a
reasonably early hour on Tuesday morning, October 23.
Nearly all the gentlemen interested or curious in such
matters, visited the extensive depots and machine shops
of the Union Pacific Railroad, and expressed their
astonishment and delight at the magnitude and adaptation
of the works, the construction of which had only been
commenced within a year from the present time.

It was a source of very general regret, that Mr. Samuel B. Reed, the efficient General Superintendent of the Road, and Engineer in Charge of Construction, was prevented, by severe illness, from showing any attention to the excursionists at Omaha, and also from accompanying them over the road. His place, however, was admirably filled by Mr. Webster Snyder, his principal assistant, aided by Mr. G. W. Frost, Major L. S. Bent, General Casement, Mr. A. A. Bean, Mr. Congdon, Mr. Gambol, and the other heads of departments.

The Chief Engineer, Gen. G. M. Dodge, who had returned from the mountains during the previous week, rendered every assistance in his power ; and the Consulting Engineer, by his timely presence, was enabled to relieve the others from much, if not all the *heavy standing around.*

THE EXCURSION TRAIN.

The excursion train consisted of nine cars drawn by two of the Company's powerful locomotives. The magnificent Directors' car, constructed by the Pittsburgh, Fort Wayne and Chicago Railroad Company for this road, was placed in the rear, and devoted to members of Congress, and other distinguished guests, who felt desirous of making a critical examination of the road and adjacent country, which they now visited for the first, and possibly the last time.

The next car forward, was the celebrated Government, or Lincoln car, the private property of Mr. Durant, and was therefore devoted principally to his own personal friends and their families.

In front of this, were four fine passenger coaches, put up at the Company's car-shops at Omaha. These were devoted to the excursionists generally. One of which, however, was occupied almost exclusively by the Elkhorn Club.

Next in order, came the mess, or cooking car, constructed also at the. Fort Wayne shops, and designed as a tender, or companion to the Directors' car. In front of this was a mail, or express car, conveniently fitted up as a refreshment saloon. And in front of all, or next to the engine, was the baggage and supply car. The engines were profusely decked with flags, and appropriate mottoes ; and the whole outfit presented a most imposing appearance, as it left the Missouri Valley, and steamed away towards the Rocky Mountains.

ALL ON BOARD.

It had been announced by Mr. Durant that the excursion train would start westward at ten in the morning. But the difficulty and delay attending the gathering together of the excursionists, prevented our departure till about twelve, when the entire party, enlarged by the civil and military authorities, members of Congress, etc., of the Territory, with their families, started westward in high spirits, to view, most of them for the first time, the great, and almost uninhabited Platte Valley, extending, as it does, in an almost direct westerly course from the Missouri River to the Rocky Mountains, a distance of six hundred miles.

The train had been supplied by Mr. Hoxie with every comfort and even luxury that the heart could wish ; and soon after starting, the guests were invited to partake of an excellent lunch, served through the cars by the attentive waiters.

THE GREAT PLATTE VALLEY.

The fine valleys of Mud Creek, and the Papillon, were passed successively, and at about two P. M., the Great Platte Valley opened to the view, and elicited an exclamation of wonder and admiration from all who now saw it for the first time.

The train—which had been ordered by Mr. Durant to proceed at a slow rate of speed, so that the excursionists could obtain a satisfactory view, not only of the surrounding beautiful country, but of the road and structures, as they passed—after halting at the fine bridge structures over the Papillon and Elkhorn Rivers, stopped a short time at the Fremont and North Bend stations, in order to give the guests an opportunity of examining the commodious depot buildings, water stations, etc., which had been constructed by the Company at intervals of fifteen or twenty miles along the line.

ARRIVAL AT COLUMBUS.

The train finally reached Columbus, the proposed end of the first day's journey, a little after night-fall, and here a new surprise awaited the party.

The train was halted immediately in front of a brilliantly illuminated encampment, which covered several acres of beautiful ground situated a few rods northward of the Columbus station buildings, and so arranged as to afford comfortable accommodations for all who wished to leave the cars and enjoy the novelty of a night's sleep in camp.

Soon after our arrival, supper was announced by the ubiquitous Hoxie, and the party found themselves comfortably seated in a large tent, and urged to partake of

substantials and luxuries, which might well have vied
with those found upon the tables of our Eastern hotels.

The irrepressible Elkhorns were seen and heard everywhere, adding life and exhilaration to the scene; and
thus an hour or two were passed in social intercourse
until the evening's entertainment was announced.

INDIAN WAR-DANCE.

This entertainment consisted of a war-dance, at a
short distance from the encampment, executed by a large
delegation of Pawnee braves, under the immediate supervision of that celebrated *Indianist*, Professor Taylor, who
had most kindly volunteered his valuable services for the
occasion; and of all the wild and hideous yells, grotesque
shapes and contortions that have ever been witnessed by
a civilized assemblage in the night-time upon the plains
this was most certainly the climax. The light of the
moon, aided slightly by that of a dim camp fire, was
barely sufficient to enable the spectators to distinguish
the features and grotesque costumes of the savage per-
formers; and the congregation of lady and gentlemen
spectators were only too glad to know that the Indians
were entirely friendly, and catering only for the amusement of the company, instead of being enemies, dancing
and gloating over their scalpless bodies. This amusement being ended, the waning moon and camp fires
admonished the excursionists that the hour for retire-
ment and rest had arrived.

Each individual, family, and party, found comfortable
tents allotted to them, well stored with soft hay mattres-
ses, buffalo robes, and blankets. Without the least dis-
order or confusion, therefore, all were soon dreaming of
the wondrous novelty of the situation; and nothing but

the howling of the distant wolf, or the subdued mutter-
ings from the Indian camp, broke the stillness of this
first night on the plains.

A MORNING SERENADE.

Before daylight, however, the more timid of the party
were startled from their slumbers by the most unearthly
whoops and yells of the Indians, who were tramping
about among the camp fires in front of the tents; and
many disordered heads, with anxious and inquiring coun-
tenances, were to be seen protruding through the aper-
tures of the tents, to ascertain whether they were to be
immediately roasted alive, or allowed a short time in
which to say their prayers, and write a few parting words
to their distant friends.

All was soon explained however, when it became known
that Mr. Durant himself, assisted by General Dodge,
Secretary Paddock, and a partially standing, but more
generally reclining committee of Elkhorns, had these
wild denizens of the plains, under the most complete control; and were only making them dance and perform this
most unique and savage morning serenade for their own
particular amusement.

Quiet was therefore soon restored, and, after a refreshing morning nap, the party was invited to partake of a sumptuous breakfast before again starting
westward.

THE TOWN OF COLUMBUS.

This goodly town of Columbus should, however, have
more than a passing notice.

It is situated near the confluence of the Loup Fork
River with the Platte, and is surrounded by one of the
finest agricultural countries in the world. Being near

the centre of the Territory, it bids fair soon to become the Capital of this embryo State. The large and valuable Pawnee reservation is situated only a few miles from the town, in the Valley of Loup Fork.

The *Credit-Foncier of America* has invested largely in town and suburban property, and promises, through its far-seeing and enterprising managers, to add much to its future growth and prosperity.

The tents were soon struck, and the pioneer train was to be seen steaming far away in the distance; after which, our excursionists leisurely resumed their places in the cars, ready for new surprises and adventures.

Many of them little dreamed, however, that one, most rare and novel in its character, was so soon to be realized.

SHAM INDIAN FIGHT.

The train halted upon a high embankment, in front of the Indian encampment, near the east end of the beautiful bridge which spans the Loup-Fork river.

The Indians, fully dressed and adorned in the war costume of the Pawnees, were in council, many of them evidently in a high state of excitement, gesticulating, whooping and yelling, in the most frantic and unearthly manner. Twenty or thirty horses stood near, ready to be mounted.

Soon a band of about thirty mounted Sioux warriors were to be seen emerging stealthily from a thicket, some distance down the river, and making their way cautiously in a circuit, as if to surround the Pawnee camp.

Our Pawnees were instantly mounted, and following their stalwart chief, with shrieks and cries of vengeance, to the attack. The shock of meeting was grand and terrific. Horses reared and plunged against each other. Indian grappled Indian, and both fell to the ground in deadly embrace. Rifles, revolvers and arrows were dis-charged apparently with deadly effect. Riderless horses, and horseless riders were to be seen roaming wildly over the plain. And all was confusion and intense excitement, until at length the victorious Pawnees brought their van-quished enemies into camp, amid the most tempestuous shouts of triumph and exultation.

All this had been but a *sham* Indian fight, between a party of Pawnee warriors, dressed in the costume of the Sioux, and an equal number of their own tribe. What then must be the terrible reality, when these ever hostile tribes meet, as they often do, in deadly conflict?

After the battle had ended, Mr. Durant distributed several hundred dollars' worth of presents among the Indians and their squaws. And it was most amusing to see these greedy savages exercise all the arts and *indianuity* of which the most civilized mind is capable, for the purpose of obtaining more than their just and proper share of the spoils. The squaws, too, were most curious in their observation of the peculiar construction of the hoop-skirts and elegant balmorals worn by our lady excursionists; and also tried by every means in their power to enlist the sympathies of these kind-hearted ladies in behalf of the young papooses hanging upon their backs.

Perhaps no better illustration could have been given of the extremes of civilized and savage life, standing face to face with each other, than the one now before us. On the one side was the track of the Union Pacific Railroad, upon which stood that great civilizer, the locomotive and train, looking westward over the Loup-Fork bridge, fifteen hundred feet in length; and in the foreground stood the group of excursionists, composed of beauty, intelligence and refinement; while, on the other hand, were grouped these uncouth savages, many of them almost in their normal state, except for the profuse display of feathers and trinkets which bedecked their persons ; low and brutal in their habits, and mentally elevated but slightly, if at all, above the level of the beasts that inhabit this vast and beautiful country with them.

But the laws of civilization are such that it must press forward ; and it is in vain that these poor ignorant creatures attempt to stay its progress by resisting inch by inch, and foot by foot, its onward march over these lovely plains, where but a few years since, they were " monarchs of all they surveyed."

The locomotive must go onward until it reaches the Rocky Mountains, the Laramie Plains, the great Salt Lake, the Sierra Nevada, and the Pacific Ocean. Lateral roads must also be built, extending in all directions from the main line, as veins from an artery, and penetrating the hunting-grounds of these worse than useless Indian tribes, until they are either driven from the face of the earth ; or forced to look for safety in the adoption of that very civilization and humanity, which they now so savagely ignore and despise.

THE TRAIN AGAIN STARTS WESTWARD.

When this most interesting exhibition of savage life and customs was ended, the excursion train started again on its westward course, passing successively the embryo towns of Silver-Creek, Lone-Tree, Grand-Island, Wood-River, Kearny, Elm-Creek, Plum-Creek, and Willow-Island. Soon after which, and at about eight P. M., it arrived at the termination of the second day's journey, a distance of two hundred and seventy-nine miles west of Omaha.

ARRIVAL AT CAMP No. 2.

Here, as at Columbus, on the previous evening, a large and brilliantly illuminated encampment had been prepared for the reception of the guests.

A military encampment had also been established during the previous day by Colonel Mizner, in command of Fort McPherson on the opposite side of the Platte, so near the excursionists' camp as to preclude any fear from the roaming bands of Indians, which were said to infest this portion of the country.

Comfortable quarters were immediately assigned to each one of the party, and very soon thereafter an elegant supper was announced, and partaken of with a gusto, known only to a party whose only sustenance for hours had been the pure bracing air of the illimitable plains.

When the excursion party left New York, it was understood that it would overtake the western end of the Union Pacific Railroad track, at or about the one hundredth meridian of longitude, some two hundred and forty-seven miles west of Omaha; and that then and there the great celebration would come off, as per invitation and programme. But here we now were, more than thirty miles west of the one hundredth meridian, and no end of track yet visible. Nothing remained for the excursionists, therefore, but to take another night's rest, and endeavor by an early start on the following morning, to overtake this long-sought-for goal, which to many of the party seemed only a myth, or most perplexing illusion.

The spacious headquarters tents, which had been hung about with transparencies, and elegantly decorated with flags for the occasion, were therefore soon bereft of their occupants, who had sought the greater retiracy of the more private quarters assigned to them; and after the establishment of a telegraph, and printing office, by means of which to communicate with the outer world, the encampment soon became as still as solitude itself, except the measured tramp of the guard or distant sentinel, whose duty it was to see that we were not molested either by friends within or foes from without.

MORNING EXERCISES.

On the following morning the camp showed signs of early life. Individuals and parties were to be seen looking about for the means of ablution and renovation.

The famous Elkhorn Club formed in line in front of their quarters, with President Dunlap and Vice-President Smith at its head, and followed in proper order by its professional *speechists, singists, cheerists, punists, jokeists, eatists, drinkists,* etc., etc., marched in a body to the banks of the Platte River, where each member underwent the pleasant operation of a wholesome *outward* application of an element to which the inner man had, from the force of circumstances, become a comparative stranger during the few preceding days.

After a hearty breakfast, the inquiry became quite general as to the programme of operations for the day. A bulletin board was therefore placed in front of headquarters, upon which the following printed announcements and orders were soon posted for general information :—

CAMP No. 2, U. P. R. R., BUFFALO Co., NEB., }
Thursday, October 25, 1866. }

SPECIAL NOTICE.

"Colonel N. A. Gestner is announced as Officer-of-the-Day. Office at headquarters tent.

Chiefs of all working and fatigue parties will immediately report to him for orders."

By Order.

CITY ORGANIZATION.

"A meeting of citizens will be held this day at the Music Stand in the Public Square, at 9 A. M., for the purpose of locating a city, the election of a Mayor, City Council, and the transaction of such other business as may be presented.

"Let there be a full attendance."

By Order.

TO THE REPRESENTATIVES OF THE PRESS.

"The Representatives of the Press are requested to meet at the Press headquarters (left wing of the dining hall), at 10 o'clock this morning."

"AN EXCURSION TRAIN will leave for the End of the Track, at 11 A. M."

THE BUFFALO HUNT.

"Gentlemen wishing to go on a buffalo or antelope hunt will please report to Captain Hollins, at headquarters. Captain H., with an experienced hunter, will accompany the party. Buffalo are said to be in abundance on the Republican, and antelope nearer camp. The party will be absent about four days. Horses and ponies will be provided."

DEPARTURE OF THE ELKHORNS.

Very much to the disappointment and regret of all parties, a large number of the officers, professors, and leading spirits of the Elkhorn Club were obliged to leave soon after breakfast, in a special train for the east. Professor Ayer, the *goutist* of the Club, remained however, and added very much to the hilarity of the party by riding about in an old one-horse wagon, driven by Major Bent; this method of locomotion being rendered necessary, as he remarked, by the unmanageableness of his *stuttering* feet.

The following dispatch was received from the Elkhorn party during the day :—

"KEARNY, *October* 25, 1866.

"DR. T. C. DURANT—

"Our eyes are filled with unaccustomed tears ; and our hearts are bowed with grief. The Elkhorns mourn for their Fawns.

"ELKHORNS."

The following reply was immediately sent :—

TO THE DEPARTED ELKHORNS.

"The better half of all our joys
Departed with the Elkhorn boys ;
To their memory we'll light the lamp,
And dance around our prairie camp.
"FAWNS."

LIST OF EXCURSIONISTS.

The first number of the *Railway Pioneer* was issued from the press during the morning, and contained, among a large variety of interesting and amusing matter, the following :

LIST OF NAMES OF THE EXCURSION PARTY—GUESTS OF THE U. P. R. R.

EXCURSION CAMP, *October* 25, 1866.

DIRECTORS AND OFFICERS OF THE U. P. R. R. COMPANY.

Thomas C. Durant, New York, Vice-President,
E. Cook, Iowa,
Sidney Dillon, New York,
C. A. Lambard, Massachusetts,   } *Directors.*
John Duff, Massachusetts,
Hon. C. T. Sherman, Ohio, Government Director.
General J. H. Simpson, Washington,
General S. R. Curtis, Iowa,   } *Government Commissioners.*
Hon. W. M. White, Connecticut.
Gen. G. M. Dodge, Iowa, Chief Engineer.
Col. Silas Seymour, New York, Consulting Engineer.
W. Snyder, Assistant Superintendent and General Freight and Ticket Agent.

Attachés :

H. M. Hoxie, in charge of steamboats.
B. F. Bunker, N. A. Gestner, in charge of special train.

G. W. Frost, Purchasing Agent.

Maj. L. S. Bent, Burnetizer.

General and Daniel Casement, in charge of track.

J. Carbutt, Photographer ; Mr. Hien, Assistant Photographer.

Great Western Light Guard Band of Chicago—A. J. Vaas, Leader.

Rosenblatt's Band of St. Joseph—H. Rosenblatt, Leader.

INVITED GUESTS.

Hon. B. F. Wade, U. S. Senator.

Hon. J. W. Patterson, U. S. Senator.

Hon. M. Welker.

Hon. W. Lawrence.

Hon. J. B. Alley and wife.

Miss Emma Alley.

Hon. R. B. Buckland.

Hon. I. T. Rogers.

Hon. R. B. Hays.

Hon. B. M. Boyer and wife.

Hon. S. E. Ancona.

Hon. J. H. Farquar and wife.

LeGrand Lockwood.

Henry B. Lockwood.

Earl of Arlie, England.

M. O'Dillon Barrot, Secretary French Legation.

Marquis Chambrun.

Mr. and Mrs. J. T. McCobb.

Miss A. M. Williams.

Horace Williams.

Wm. Leighton.

Mrs. J. H. Simpson.

Miss Minnie Simpson.

Miss Graff.

J. T. Tuttle, M.D.

J. E. Sherman.

Miss M. H. Sherman.

Rev. Dr. G. F. Wiswell and wife.

B. D. Stewart.

Miss H. R. Stewart.

J. R. Duff.

Miss Duff.

Miss Hall.

Rev. I. H. Tuttle, D.D., and wife.

Col. E. D. Taylor.

Miss Kate Offley.

S. J. Jones, Surgeon, U. S. N.

Gen. J. H. Bates.

Hon. Augustus Schell.

Rev. W. R. Brown.

John Crerar.

Mr. and Mrs. George Francis Train and maid.

Mrs. George T. M. Davis.

Miss Sallie Clark.

Mrs. J. S. Polhemus.

Miss M. S. Dodge.

Mr. and Mrs. W. H. Bailhache.

Hon. Thomas F. Plunkett.

Hon. G. B. Senter.

G. A. Benedict.

Col. Thomas Dimmick.

Ezra H. Baker.

Miss E. H. Baker.

Miss Bugbee.

Dr. F. Plummer.

Isaac S. Waterman.

Mr. and Mrs. J. H. Connelly.

H. M. Smith.

Col. William Osborn.

Mrs. R. A. Park.

Mrs. A. P. Clark.

Capt. St. Albe.

S. R. Wells.

H. M. Kinsley.
Dr. and Mrs. S. L. Sprague.
J. A. Gilden.
E. T. Watkins.
Wm. Hilton.
Joseph Medill.
Col. A. W. Johnson.
John Potts.
J. H. Bowen.
R. M. McHenry.
T. W. Fabens.
Mr. and Mrs. W. H. Painter.
C. F. Atkinson.
Josiah Hastings.
F. H. Hall.
C. B. Hazeltine.
B. P. Hazeltine.
Perry H. Smith, Jr.
Col. B. H. Jenks.
Dr. H. B. VanDeventer.
R. D. Hicks.
E. Reily.
W. G. Mendenhall.
Mr. and Mrs. D. W. Kilbourne.
George E. Kilbourne.
Mr. and Mrs. R. Harris.
Ira P. Bowen.
F. S. Lathrop.
A. N. Allen, M.D.
F. W. Hinsdale.
Mrs. S. Seymour.
J. M. Seymour.
Franklin C. White.
Thomas H. Cuthell.
S. P. Holmes.
Luther Kountze.
J. W. Miller.
William L. Woods.
Major Hennings.
Mr. Winter.
Capt. John B. Turner.
W. H. Ferry.
Perry H. Smith.

George L. Dunlap.
E. B. Talcott.
Col. J. H. Howe.
John C. Gault.
Isaac B. Howe.
John V. Ayer.
George M. Pullman.
Hiram Wheeler.
Charles H. Hapgood.
Robert T. Lincoln.
Norman Williams.
John M. Rountree.
Hon. H. B. Curtis.
Henry L. Curtis.
Dr. J. M. Buckingham.
Charles T. Sherman, Jr.
Dr. R. D. Hicks.
S. Lathrop.
Miss Hattie V. Lathrop.
A. Winton.
Mr. and Mrs. J. W. Balch.
C. F. Atkinson.
Rev. W. R. Brown.
T. R. Montgomery.
L. L. Harman.
George R. Smith, P. M., Omaha.
Gen. G. M. O'Brien and lady.
Dr. Alexander, Medical Director.
St. A. D. Balcombe and lady.
Major Bird.
George L. Miller.
E. B. Taylor.
F. M. McDonough.
Judge C. Baldwin.
H. C. Nutt, Esq., and lady.
Mrs. Gen. Dodge and daughter.
Miss Julia M. Dodge.
Mrs. H. M. Hoxie.
Mrs. G. W. Frost.
Miss C. M. Frost.
Miss A. J. Shaw.
Mrs. D. T. Casement.
John Jones.

Hon. A. Saunders, Governor of Nebraska.

Hon. J. M. Thayer and lady, and Hon. T. W. Tipton, U. S. Senators elect.

Hon. William Kellogg, Chief Justice of Nebraska.

Major-General Phillip St. George Cooke (commanding Department of the Platte) and Staff.

Hon. A. S. Paddock, and lady, Secretary of Nebraska.

Major Cushing, Chief Commissary of the Platte.

Col. J. K. Mizner, (Fort McPherson), lady and sister.

Lieut. Yates, Second Cavalry, United States Army.

Lieut. A. S. Adams, Second Cavalry, U. S. A.

C. L. Jenkins, in charge *Railway Pioneer* Printing Establishment.

J. Shepherd, Superintendent United States Express Company.

"Giles," Editor *Bugle*, Council Bluffs, Iowa.

W. F. Burke, Editor *Nonpareil*, Council Bluffs, Iowa.

The following account of a public meeting held in the hollow square, in the centre of the encampment, is also taken from the *Railway Pioneer :—*

PUBLIC MEETING.

"A public meeting was held in the square this A. M., pursuant to notice. Hon. Alvin Saunders, of Nebraska, was called to the chair, and appointed secretary.

"Brief and appropriate addresses were made by Senators Wade of Ohio, Patterson of New Hampshire, Tipton of Nebraska, Hon. Mr. Lawrence of Ohio, Hon. John B. Alley of Mass., Dr. Wisewell, and others.

Mr. Lawrence of Ohio, offered the following resolutions which were unanimously adopted :

" *Whereas,* An excursion party of ladies and gentlemen from various places in both hemispheres, started from New York city on the evening of October 15th, 1866, to visit the Union Pacific Railroad so far as finished, to a point west of the hundreth meridian of west longitude ; and

" *Whereas,* Said excursionists, with many others who have joined them on the route, have this day reached said destina-

5

tion, at a point on said railroad two hundred and seventy-nine miles west of Omaha ; and

" *Whereas*, Said excursionists have passed over all or parts of the following railways, and lines of travel, to-wit :— the New Jersey Central Railroad ; the Allentown Railroad ; the Pennsylvania Central Railroad ; the Pittsburg, Fort Wayne and Chicago Railroad ; the Chicago, Burlington and Quincy Railroad ; the Chicago and Northwestern Railroad ; the Des Moines Valley Railroad; the Hannibal and St. Joseph Railroad ; the steamers Denver and Colorado from St. Joseph to Omaha ; and the Union Pacific Railroad.

" And *Whereas*, This excursion was designed to celebrate the formal opening of the Union Pacific Railroad—so far as finished—for travel and the transportation of commerce to and from the great interior of, and across, the North American continent, with its vast agricultural and mineral resources.

" *Resolved*, That this excursion party here assembled in the centre of this vast continent, now offer up our heartfelt gratitude and thanks to Almighty God for His manifold blessings, among which we enumerate that country subject to the jurisdiction of the United States of America, republican institutions, civil and religious liberty, the freedom of speech and the press, a Union unbroken and indestructible, with all the material resources necessary for the comfort of mankind in a high and rapidly advancing state of development; and with a vast net-work of railroads and telegraphs essential not only to our national prosperity and the interests of all our people; but also to the civilization and commerce of the world, including among the most important of them all, that vast work—The Union Pacific Railroad.

" *Resolved*, That it is the deliberate opinion of this excursion party that our nation and the world have abundant reason to rejoice that the Union Pacific Railroad was projected, and is in successful progress to completion, and we congratulate mankind at the success of this magnificent enterprise.

"*Resolved,* That our thanks are due and are hereby tendered to the Union Pacific Railroad Company for their energy and enterprise in the rapid construction of their railroad, as well as for their excursion, celebrating thus far the opening of their railroad.

"*Resolved,* That Thomas C. Durant, the Vice-President and General Manager of the Union Pacific Railroad Company, and his subordinates in its direction, deserve and have our sincere thanks for this excursion and for the energy and enterprise they have displayed in organizing and conducting it ; and for the splendid and unsurpassed accommodations provided for the convenience and comfort of the excursionists.

"*Resolved,* That our thanks are due and hereby tendered to the Central Transportation Company for the splendid ' Palace Sleeping Cars,' so generously furnished by them for this Excursion,

"*Resolved,* That our thanks are due and are hereby tendered to George M. Pullman, Esq., of Chicago, for his liberal hospitality and generosity in furnishing the magnificent train of 'Palace Sleeping Cars,' for our party over the Chicago and Quincy Railroad, and for the sumptuous entertainment provided at his instance by the prince of caterers, ' Kinsley,' of Chicago.

"*Resolved,* That our thanks are due and are hereby tendered to Governor Alvin Saunders of Nebraska, for the cordial welcome to this Territory which he extended to our party at Omaha; and to the Mayor and Council of Omaha, and to the people of that city for the hospitalities and the splendid entertainment given us during our stay at that flourishing capital.

"*Resolved,* That our thanks are in like manner extended to the several Railroad Companies of the lines of road over which we have passed, and to the officers and crews of the steamers 'Denver,' and 'Colorado,' on the Missouri River, for the excellent accommodations and safe and speedy transportation furnished by them each and all for our large party.

> Hon. WM. LAWRENCE, of Ohio.
> " E. H. BAKER, Mass.
> " A. C. SCHELL, New York.
> " JOHN H. FARQUAR, Indiana.
> Col. R. H. JENKS, Penn.
> JOSEPH MEDILL, Illinois.
> Gen. J. M. THAYER, Nebraska."

END OF THE TRACK FOUND AT LAST.

At eleven o'clock the party started, as per announcement, in the train for the end of the track, which was finally found some eight or ten miles still farther west.

On the way to the end of the track, we met one of Mr. Durant's foraging parties, on horseback, laden with antelope and other game for the table. This party reported that the party which had previously been sent out to hunt for buffalo, had been quite successful, but unfortunately, as they were returning to camp, they met with a strong party of Indians, who took their buffaloes from them, and spared their lives only on condition that they should never be found again upon their hunting-grounds.

Some hours were spent by the party in the vicinity of the end of the track, in observing the process adopted by those great *trackists*, General and Daniel Casement, in laying the track, subsisting their men, distributing materials, etc. Photographic pictures were also taken by the celebrated *Viewist*, Professor Carbutt of Chicago, of the construction train; and also various groupings of the officers of the road and excursionists. The *shootists* of the party amused themselves by firing at marks, or other objects on the distant bluffs and river. Senator Wade of Ohio, distinguished himself by making several fine shots with the little Ballard rifle, which had recently done such excellent execution among the elk and antelope of the Rocky Mountains ; and he finally became so much attached to the rifle, that he would not allow his photograph to be taken without holding it in his hand. A general *abandon* seemed to pervade the entire party; and every one appeared inclined to yield to the influence of the quiet and majestic repose, which reigned supreme over all the vast plains.

DINNER IN CAMP.

A sumptuous game dinner awaited the hungry excursionists on their return to the camp during the latter part of the day, as will be seen by referring to the following bill of fare, a printed copy of which was found beside the plate of each guest :—

UNION PACIFIC RAILROAD EXCURSION.

BILL OF FARE.

PLATTE CITY, NEBRASKA. }
HOXIE HOUSE, *October* 25, 1866. }

ROAST.

| Beef. | Mutton. | Lamb, with Green Peas. | Brazen Ox. |
| | Tongue. | Maccaroni a la Italian. | |

BOILED.

| Mutton. | Tongue. | Ham. | Corned Beef. |

GAME.

| Antelope, Roasted. | Sardine Salid. | Roman Goose. |
| | Chinese Duck. | |

VEGETABLES.

Peas. Tomatoes. Asparagus. Mashed Potatoes.

RELISHES.

London Club Sauce. Worcestershire Sauce. Horrey Sauce.
Pickles. Pineapple Cheese. Swiss Cheese.

PASTRY.

Pies. Strawberries. Damson. Peach. Cherry.

FRUITS.

Apples. Pineapples.

To which should be added, as representing the principal feature of the unpublished wine list :

THE UNION PACIFIC RAILROAD,

VERZENAY.

Vᴇ MAX SUTAINE ET CIE.

T. W. & G. D. BAYAUD,

Sole Agents for United States and Canada.

The following special notices appeared in the evening edition of the *Railway Pioneer :*

SPECIAL NOTICE.

A concert will be given this evening at Bunker Hall, by the celebrated Northwestern Band of Chicago. Tickets for sale at all principal hotels, and at the door.

Doors open at 7½ o'clock ; performance to commence at 8 o'clock precisely.

Seven locomotives were at the depot in this city, this morning.

Eastern papers desiring an exchange with the *Pioneer*, will be placed upon our exchange list by publishing our prospectus three times in their daily and one month in their weekly issues.

A photograph gallery and a first-class barber-shop are among the recent additions to our embryo city.

The excursion train for the end of the track left promptly at 11 A. M. The excursionists witnessed the laying of about 800 feet of track during their brief stay of half an hour. Casement's men are putting down the iron at the unprecedented rate of a mile and a half per day. So we go, on our march to the Pacific!

FIRE-WORKS ON THE PLAINS.

The principal attraction of the evening was the magnificent display of fire-works from the stand in the centre of the camp, under the immediate supervision of those distinguished pyrotechnists, *Professors* Snyder and Seymour.

Rockets, falling stars, golden rain, serpents, magazines, Roman candles, together with all sorts of eccentric wheels, and other ingenious contrivances, were to be seen and heard, shooting and whizzing through the air for more than an hour, much to the amazement, no doubt, of the distant savages and wild beasts, who might happen to be the witnesses of this first exhibition of the kind in the great Platte Valley.

Later in the evening, the grand concert at Bunker Hall came off, as per special notice. This was followed by an interesting lecture upon phrenology, delivered by that great *Bumpist*, Professor Wells, which was most amusingly illustrated by a reference to the head of Mr. George Francis Train, the *humorist* of the party.

The party finally retired to rest in the best possible humor with themselves, and their hospitable entertainers.

HOMEWARD BOUND.

On the following morning all was commotion at an early hour in the encampment, in consequence of the following bulletin, which had been issued by Mr. Durant:—

UNION PACIFIC RAILROAD, HEADQUARTERS, CAMP No. 2, }
Friday, Oct. 26, 1866.   }

Special Train No. 1 will leave with the Government Commissioners at 7½ A. M. to examine thirty miles of the road.

Special Train No. 2 will leave at 8 A. M., and will unite with Train No. 1, thirty-five miles east of this camp, arriving in Omaha at 7 P. M.

Ample provisions have been made for those of the guests desiring to take the stage from Council Bluffs to the western terminus of the Chicago and Northwestern Railroad. The Iowa stage ride will occupy but ten hours' time, and the trip by rail thence to Chicago will be in Pullman's magnificent sleeping-cars.

Guests desiring to remain can use their excursion tickets during the two weeks next ensuing.

Parties preferring to return via St. Joseph will please take the steamer Denver at Omaha. The tickets issued for this excursion are good for the return trip on the Hannibal and St. Joseph, the Chicago, Burlington and Quincy, and Pittsburg Fort Wayne and Chicago, and Pennsylvania Railroads by making application to Mr. Creighton at Pittsburg. Those desiring to return via Michigan Southern, Lake Shore and New York Central Railroads can do so by giving notice of their intention at Omaha.

T. C. DURANT.

Professor Carbutt was now in great demand. Everybody wanted to be taken just as they appeared at the breaking up of the camp. The Professor finally succeeded in obtaining some excellent groupings, as well as camp and landscape views before the train started eastward.

At about ten A. M., the whistle of the engine gave the signal for the start homeward. Although every one seemed delighted with the trip, and satisfied to return, yet many longing eyes could be observed looking backwards, as if, other duties permitting, they would prefer, having started the other way, not to return until they had obtained a view of the Rocky Mountains, and the fabulous mines of treasure which are hidden in their embrace.

ONE HUNDREDTH MERIDIAN.

The train was halted for nearly an hour directly opposite the monument designating the point where the line of the road crosses the one hundreth meridian of longitude, for the purpose of enabling Professor Carbutt to photograph some views representing the excursion train, with groupings of Government officers, members of Congress, Directors of the road, and excursionists, coming to this point *from the west*.

This being accomplished, and the train which had been placed at the disposal of the Government Commissioners having been attached, the excursion train sped onward again at the rate of thirty miles an hour, stopping only for wood and water, until it reached a point about four miles below Kearny.

PRAIRIE-DOG CITY.

Here the train halted for nearly two hours, for the purpose of enabling the excursionists to pay their respects to the inhabitants of by far the largest town through which they had passed since leaving Chicago. This pleasing duty had been in contemplation as the train passed westward two days previously, and was prevented only by the lateness of the hour.

This town occupies an area of about twenty-five square miles, and the railroad track passes through its centre. The visit was evidently a surprise to the vast number of its quiet and peaceful inhabitants, and no preparations had therefore been made, as at Omaha, for the reception of their distinguished guests.

Their native politeness and curiosity, however, induced many of them, soon after the arrival of the train, to peep out of their doors and chatter an incoherent welcome ; but the salutation which awaited them was not of a kind calculated to encourage a protracted acquaintance of even this unsatisfactory nature, and all civilities were therefore soon at an end.

The *huntists* of the party soon spread themselves over several acres of the town, in the hope of securing a few specimens as mere matter of curiosity. Several hundred shots were fired ; and, if the accounts of our brave *huntists* may be credited, at least one half that number had been killed ; but by some strange fatality or illusion, on arriving at the spot where the ball was seen to strike them, they were not there. Only one was brought to the train, and he, after being subjected to the critical examination of all the excursionists, was turned over to the cook ; and the last that was seen of him, he was rapidly disappearing before the steady gaze of Professor Ayer, who protested meantime that, " it had come to a pretty pass, if this grand excursion was reduced to such a strait that its guests were obliged to subsist on *prairie-dog.*"

These prairie-dog cities are a great curiosity in their way. They generally occupy the most dry and elevated table lands of the Plains. The Union Pacific Railroad passes through or near many of them.

The harmless little animals are somewhat the nature, and about one-half the size of the common ground hog or woodchuck. They burrow in the ground, and evidently subsist, without water, upon grass and roots in the near vicinity of their town, as they are never seen far away from it.

Tradition, as well as more modern authority, insists that their apartments are occupied conjointly with owls and rattlesnakes ; but of the truth of this, deponent prefers remaining silent, remarking only, that he has seen, and killed prairie-dogs, owls and rattlesnakes, in the immediate vicinity of the same town.

FIRE ON THE PRAIRIES.

Reaching the lower end of the Platte Valley a little after dark, the excursionists were electrified by what, to most of them, was their first view of a night-fire on the prairies.

The train was immediately halted, and time given for all to drink their fill of the sublime spectacle. The flames extended in an unbroken line a distance of from fifteen to twenty miles ; and one end of the belt of fire was so near, that we could feel the heat, and distinctly hear the roaring and crackling of the devouring element, as it swept over the plains with almost railroad velocity, and shot up its forked flames into the sombre smoky sky.

"What surprise awaits us next? " "When, and where will these wonders end ? " " We did not know that this was in the programme ! " exclaimed the excursionists, little dreaming that Mr. Durant had given private instructions upon this very subject, as the train passed up the valley two days before.

RETURN TO OMAHA.

The train arrived at Omaha at about ten in the evening. Carriages were in waiting to convey the excursionists either to the Hernden House, or the steamer "Denver," where an excellent supper, and good quarters awaited them. And all retired to rest, "perchance to dream " of the "loved ones at home," whose happy faces would soon be seen again ; and whose ears would soon be tingling with the most romantic and improbable tales, of Indian fights and war-dances; adventures with the Elkhorns; camping-out on the great plains almost in sight of the Rocky Mountains; living on buffalo and antelope meat; prairie-dog towns; fire on the prairies in the night time, etc., etc.

DEPARTURE OF EXCURSIONISTS EASTWARD.

On the following morning the continuity of the party was broken, after many hearty hand-shakings, and affectionate adieus, by the departure of a large number *via* the overland route, by stage and rail, for Chicago and the East, under the charge of Mr. C. A. Lambard, one of the managing Directors of the Union Pacific Railroad. These were met at the western end of the railroad track by the officers of the Chicago and Northwestern Railroad Company, and a delegation from the Elkhorn Club, who accompanied them to Chicago, and entertained them on the way in the most princely style.

The balance of the party remained at Omaha till Sunday morning, and then left by the steamer Denver for St. Joseph, in charge of Mr. Hoxie and Mr. Simmonds.

Before starting, however, the crowd was called to the land side of the boat by Mr. John V. Ayer of Chicago, and Major Wm. M. White, and invited to unite in three rousing *Elkhorn* cheers for Mr. Durant, who was just retiring from the boat, after having bid adieu to the excursionists. These were given with a hearty good will, in *loudly suppressed silence*, thus: H—sh! H—sh!! H—sh!!! *Tiger*, H—sh!!!! and then the steamer rounded to, and moved majestically down the river.

Mr. Durant remained at Omaha, and on the line of the road, several days after the departure of the excursionists; during which time he received frequent dispatches, informing him of their uniterrupted progress eastward, and safe arrival home.

Thus ended the most important and successful celebration of the kind, that has ever been attempted in the world; and it is believed, that its favorable effect upon the progress of the greatest work of the age, will be felt for many years to come.

IX.

NEW YORK, *Feb.* 1, 1867.

The following extract from the Chicago *Tribune*,
giving an account of the public reception given to the
excursionists on their return through that city, together
with the speech of Senator Wade and others, on the
occasion, affords most satisfactory evidence that the
anticipations of the railroad company, with reference
to the favorable effects of the excursion upon the
public mind, will be more than realized:—

UNION PACIFIC RAILROAD.

RETURN OF THE EXCURSIONISTS TO CHICAGO.

*Formal Reception—Meeting at the Opera House—Address of Welcome
by Mayor Rice—Replies by Director Lambard and Senator
Wade.*

The returned excursionists from the Far West, over the route
of the Union Pacific Railroad, were formally welcomed yesterday
back to our city. The Committee of Reception, whose names
were published in our issue of yesterday, met the excursionists at
the Tremont House at nine o'clock in the morning, and escorted
them around the city. A tug was chartered in which the party
visited the crib at the other end of the lake tunnel, then sailed up
the river, inspecting those portions of the city which lie along its
variegated banks. Flint & Thompson's elevator, and one or two

other objects of special interest, were halted at, and the party entertained with a description of the modes of doing business which obtain in our young giant city. The tug having performed its duty, the party proceeded to the Board of Trade rooms, and tarried a few moments; there were, however, no speeches made, those being reserved for the formal reception of the afternoon which was given at the Opera House.

At two o'clock the doors of the Opera House were thrown open, and the few who were waiting in anticipation of that act walked in. A little later came Vaas' Light Guard Band, preceding a delegation from the Board of Trade. They entered the hall, and took their places in the orchestra, and while playing the overture—a selection from Massaniello—the citizens came. The attendance was not large, but eminently respectable. Many of our oldest citizens were there, but the great mass of the business world was too much occupied to be able to spare an afternoon on so short a notice. The lower part of the house was nearly filled, and a few ladies and gentlemen occupied the balcony circle.

The platform was occupied by the excursionists, the Committee of Reception, and a few other prominent citizens. The scenes were thrown open to the extreme rear, exposing the full depth of the magnificent stage.

INTRODUCTORY.

Hon. J. B. RICE, Mayor of Chicago, called the assembly to order, and delivered the following address :

" LADIES AND GENTLEMEN :

" I was very much gratified this morning when I was informed by one of our citizens that I should be permitted here this day to speak a word of welcome to the ladies and gentlemen who have just returned, and who have been on an excursion to the Far West, and are back now in the city. It is very gratifying to me, as the Mayor of the city, to find this demonstration made here to receive with welcome and heartfelt kindness these gentlemen who are so earnestly enlisted in improving our country, in opening our great thoroughfares by which cultivation, commerce, civilization, and Christianization shall pervade all parts of our common country. [Applause.]

" But little more than one week has elapsed since the ladies and gentlemen, that are here, as your guests, left Chicago for the Far West by railway. Since that time they have been in the midst of the lodges of the Pawnee Indians who are scattered on the boundless and fertile, but uncultivated prairies of our country. This party is called a party of excursionists, but they are really a party of men of energy and ability, with minds to conceive and genius and talent to execute this great national work which is to connect this city of Chicago with the Pacific Ocean. [Applause.] Where could they expect or where will they receive a more heartfelt welcome than they will in Chicago? [Great applause.] Not for the pecuniary gain alone to commerce and to agriculture, but for those higher qualities by which our whole race is to be benefited in mind as well as in body, and which only wait the completion of the work which they have undertaken and are carrying on so successfully. It is no part of mine, being entirely ignorant of what has been done, to explain to you the occurrences and the results of this excursion, this formal opening of so large a portion of the eastern end of the great railway line now completed, I believe, two hundred and seventy-five miles beyond Omaha. Not many of us know even what Omaha is. We will hear. In the first place I will announce to you some resolutions that have been passed, after due consideration, by many of our most eminent citizens, some of whom were in the company. These will be read to you. After these have been read, I will introduce to you some of the men who have been there to see, and who will tell you what has been done and what is going to be done, and when it will be done. I call on Mr. Rountree to read the resolutions."

THE RESOLUTIONS.

"J. M. Rountree, Esq., then read the following as the resolutions which had been adopted, and were submitted to the meeting for its action. They were unanimously adopted on motion of the Mayor:

" In view of the appreciation the citizens of Chicago have always entertained for enterprises which tend to the development of the resources of the country, and to our power, wealth, and unity as a people, rendering us consolidated at home and the special objects of admiration abroad, we recognize in the construction and opening of the Union Pacific Railroad another great achievement, reflecting vast credit upon the American people, binding together by, we trust, indissoluble bonds, the hitherto widely separated districts and peoples, outlets for central wealth, avenues for new enterprise, and another great artery through which shall flow boundless wealth and prosperity to our city. Therefore, be it

"*Resolved,* That the city of Chicago does hereby tender to the Managers of the Union Pacific Railroad, and the excursionists who have celebrated the formal opening of that road, its most cordial and hearty welcome.

"*Resolved,* That we esteem the projection and prospective completion of the Union Pacific Railroad, a matter of vital interest to our city, securing to us the most direct, cheapest and convenient mode of transit from one section to another across our vast continent, rendering Chicago the most prominent point on their great line of communication from seaboard to seaboard, and the principal *entrepôt* of ever increasing and multiform products of the vast region which this national highway traverses.

"*Resolved,* That, in the name and in behalf of the citizens of Chicago, we cordially endorse and heartily support the action of the National Legislature, which has loaned the public credit to aid private capital and enterprise in building the gigantic work of national utility and necessity; and we hope and trust the same public spirit which has actuated Congress in behalf of the Union

Pacific Railway will be exhibited to aid the proposed improvement of the inter-State water way-from the Mississippi to the Atlantic seaboard, believing that such pecuniary assistance will be repaid to the Government one hundred fold in the development of material naval and military resources of our country.

"*Resolved*, That our thanks are due and are hereby tendered to the proprietors and managers of this signal enterprise, assuring them of our highest appreciation of its magnitude, and for the skill, boldness, and ability which projected, and the marvellous rapidity with which it is being carried forward to completion."

REPLY OF HON. O. A. LAMBARD.

Mayor RICE—I will call now upon one of these men who are engaged in this noble national work, and in doing so I again offer them the hearty welcome of the people of Chicago. I call upon the Hon. Charles A. Lambard, of Boston, one of the Directors of the Pacific Railroad. Mr. LAMBARD spoke as follows:

"As a Director of the Union Pacific Railroad Company, I feel bound to say one word to you in response to this cordial welcome, for Mr. Durant, our Vice-President, who is kept away from us by sickness. In his behalf, then, and in behalf of the Union Pacific Railroad Company, let me thank you for this kind reception. Let me return thanks here in a public manner for the many kindnesses we have received in the West. Wherever we have been we have received the greatest kindness and the most lavish hospitality from all your citizens. Indeed, sir, the devices and ingenuity with which they have insured our comfort, safety, and happiness over these long lines of railroad, have excited the admiration and wonder of our friends. No men educated in a country less magnificent in resources or less expansive and liberal in influence, could conceive or do more for stranger friends; no men less learned in nature's learning could have devised the *mise en scene* we have so thankfully beheld, and so successfully carried out a plan to develop it. In regard to this subject, and in relation to the great enterprise which we have been more than seven hundred miles west of your city to celebrate its partial completion, I will say, it is an enterprise more grand in its conception than any which has yet been completed or conjectured. I do not propose to make any very serious remarks in behalf of the excursionists, but let me say they never will forget your city of Chicago, and the Chicago and Northwestern Railroad Company, and its gentlemanly officers ; we will never forget the Chicago, Burlington and Quincy Railroad. They will never forget you, Pullman, and you, Kinsley. (Great applause.) These excursionists, Mr. Mayor, consisting, as they do, of gentlemen from almost every State of the Union, men of all professions, men holding high positions in the gift of the Government, men and women of judgment, will carry back to their homes new ideas of the greatness and the magnificence of this section of our country. Such excursions cannot but be beneficial in their influence upon us all. Let me again, sir, thank you for these pleasant hospitalities, and give way to other speakers."

SPEECH OF HON. B. F. WADE.

The Chairman then introduced Honorable B. F. Wade of Ohio, as a gentleman who had seen the country over which the party had travelled and would tell them what he thought about it.

Mr. WADE, on being introduced to the audience was received with loud and long continued applause, and upon its subsidence spoke as follows :

" MR. MAYOR, LADIES AND GENTLEMEN :—

" I feel entirely inadequate to express to this assemblage the feelings which I entertain upon the subject under consideration. I have looked over the map of the whole country for a good many years, and at an early period of my study of the geography of our country and its history I was impressed deeply with the importance of this location, Chicago—and about thirty-two years ago I visited this city, or the site where the city now stands, for at that period there was no city here—there were a few rude buildings, and some gentlemen, attracted by the location and prospective importance of the place, interested in its future building up, and, like myself, believing it might grow into a great city. I attended, I recollect, a court here at that time, but there were hardly any inhabitants and very little to do in the court. I cannot describe the condition of this place at that time. I have been over the city to-day, and endeavored to recollect the sites where the important transactions were, even where the Court House stood ; but I am entirely unable now to form any definite opinion where the place was, and so of all the rest of the city. We have all heard of the wonderful and amazing growth of this city ; of the great, bold enterprise of its inhabitants—the whole country is deeply impressed with these sentiments, but, sir, it takes the presentation of the reality before us to enable us to understand the full power of your operations here. [Applause.] I have been amazed to-day, as I passed through your thorough-fares and viewed the wonderful progress that has been made in that short period. I believe that to-day you constitute a city, third in point of population, and first, I may say, in point of enterprise, upon this continent—[applause]—and I doubt whether you yourselves understand the full importance of the position on this continent which you occupy. I am sure, sir, until I passed through this excursion, I had really no conception of the importance of this point, Chicago, and, what is still more important, of the vastness and richness of the great country that lies west of you, and which is bound to contribute in the future, so much to build up the second, if not the first city upon this continent. [Applause.] I have always been a strenuous advocate for a railway communication between the Atlantic and Pacific Oceans. I have never doubted that it was a political as well as a commercial necessity, without which I do not believe that our great and glorious republic could be amplified and grow to its full dimensions. I have always been willing, as a member of the National Legislature, to do almost anything that would encourage our enterprising men to engage in this great enterprise—so great, sir, that the minds of our most courageous capitalists were almost appalled at its magnitude; and its importance was still greater than its magnitude. But, I have been over the ground, and as I passed over it, sir, looking out of the car windows and endeavoring to view every acre of the ground we passed, of the most fertile character I have ever seen, I have realized that there was nothing in the East that at all compares with it. Its capabilities exceed the imagination of any man, and we can hardly arrive by our imaginations to the importance of this great and fertile country, when it shall be covered with a dense and enterprising population, and all those fertile acres cultivated, even as the land is now cultivated in the Eastern States, and the whole of its agricultural wealth is to find its outlet through this great city. [Applause.] And that, sir, is only the commencement of it. Its agricultural wealth and productions are nothing compared to the mineral wealth lying hidden now in the mountains of that region. Why, sir, to speak of the political necessity, some men have talked about the disunion of these States. I never was one who believed in that, because I have never seen where the Almighty had erected a barrier sufficient to divide our nation into parts. [Applause.] You may look to the Gulf of Mexico, and to all our extreme southern boundary; you may traverse that line up to Canada, and even there you will find no adequate boundary. [Great applause.] You may go west from the Atlantic Ocean, traversing these vast fertile plains over which we travelled, and you will find no place for an-international boundary line. No secessionist nor disunionist can go over the ground and designate the line where disunion could possibly take place. [Applause.] I never believed the thing possible, and with a genial people, homogeneous in all their sentiments, their habits, their education, all, as it were, one family, for any man to suppose that there is anything that can finally rend them asunder, is utterly preposterous. I mean to the crest of the Rocky Mountains, for there, in my judgment, is the only place where any separation could by any possibility take place. And when I contemplate that and see that vast region beyond, rich as the other in agricultural capabilities, and infinitely richer in the material wealth, and peopled too by the same class of people, still, sir, I might fear that ambition might conceive the idea that beyond the Rocky Mountains, on the Pacific coast, a great and prosperous nation, separate from us, might be built up, and when I contemplate that, sir, I think I see the necessity of intimate connections with that people by commerce, by social relations, and all those ties that bind nations together. [Applause.] Not believing that there is any danger of such a thing, for, for the honor of that great people over there be it said, they have given us no intimation that there is any design to separate themselves from the rising and prospective glories of this great republic. [Applause.] But, sir, it is a dictate of prudence politically to cultivate the most intimate relations with that people, and use every facility for connecting ourselves most closely with them. How, sir, should this be done? Man's ingenuity has invented no other way except the all-efficient instrumentality of the railway. And that is sufficient to bind nations together this day infinitely stronger than the people of the old time were capable of. Therefore, sir, I do honor to all those who, either through patriotism or the far-reaching knowledge of their own interests, are taking in hand to expend their capital, their thought, and their labor on this great enterprise. And as we proceeded west over those vast plains, and found what the energy of those men had done, it filled our minds with the greatest degree of admiration. As the gentleman who preceded me has said, there was no man among us whose heart did not warm toward the men who engaged their fortunes in this great enterprise. They have prosecuted it with an energy that astonished me, whether it did others or not. I had no idea that this road was creeping along with such facility toward its western termination; and when I saw it I felt glad that all the votes I have ever given in Congress, having any connection with this great enterprise, have been to aid it. [Applause.] I labored to have it done, long before it was. There was a time preceding the war—for this great work has been in contemplation for a good many years—that we fought this thing persistently, but without success; we could not get it through Congress. We sent out surveyors to prospect and estimate the cost of the different roads through the Rocky Mountains and on to the Pacific coast, and they reported that it would cost a hundred millions of dollars to establish this road there, and men thought this sum so great that no nation could afford to engage in the enterprise. You all know the arguments used in Congress against it. It was extravagant, it was enormous, it would bankrupt the nation to undertake it, yet a private company of individuals, aided a little by the Government, have gone on and rendered it not only possible, but have, in a great measure, accomplished the work. [Applause.] As the gentleman who preceded me stated, we traversed the road seven hundred miles west of this place, into the very heart and centre of the continent, and there we found them going on almost as fast as man could walk. Indeed I did not know at one time if we should be able to get to the end of it, for I will say that they are prosecuting it with an unabated energy, and with a unity of purpose that is perfectly amazing. Every workman knows his place—every one is as busy as he can be—the work goes perceptibly on while you stand there viewing it; and, sir, this is most honorable to those gentlemen who have this great work in charge. I tell you that five years will not elapse before you may take the cars here and go to San Francisco in four days. [Applause.] And then think of the developments of that great country which will be disclosed. How is it now, sir, in your Rocky Mountain region, a region so remote and so little known, that ten years ago, I recollect, in Congress, when we undertook to divide it up into Territories, we were puzzled most of all to fix the boundaries, because we did not know where they would run, and, if you look in our work you will find that we have bounded them on the west "by the crest of the Rocky Mountains, wherever that might be." We knew not if there was any gold or other minerals

worth looking after there. These, however, the energy and
enterprise of our age have disclosed, and the question now is, how
shall the wealth of those regions be developed for the advantage
of the nation and the benefit of the world at large? I will say
one thing here, by way of digression, that there are those who
look upon the public debt consequent upon this work with great
apprehension, but such gentlemen have not been of these excursionists. [Applause.] They have not looked to the amazing
resources of this Government, agricultural, mineral, and otherwise. Now, just think for one moment what amounts of gold
and silver have been dug out of these mountains under all
the disadvantages of having no great mode of communication,
when men had to drag their heavy and ponderous instruments for
getting out these minerals over thousands of miles of untracked
territory, and yet, sir, they have dug out those precious metals by
hundreds of millions. Now, think of the vast chain of mountains, extending from the north of Mexico to the remotest north,
running through this great Republic from end to end, and all full
of these precious metals, and think when this railway shall be
accomplished there, when these great and ponderous instruments
so necessary to develop those minerals, shall be taken there by the
speed of the railway, and that great mineral region shall be
exposed to the enterprise of the American people everywhere with
such ease and facility—where the workmen may be fed by railway communication—where all their wants can be so easily
supplied—imagine, if you can, the immense wealth that will be
developed almost instantly when the railway reaches those regions, and then doubt, if you can, the ability of this nation to encounter any debt whatever. [Applause.] And
another thing occurs to me that I have no doubt will take
place the moment this great thoroughfare reaches the Pacific
Ocean; the whole course of trade and commerce will be changed
by which all nations, ancient and modern, have sought the
great and rich countries of the East. China and India will
be reached in one-half, nay one-third the time we reach them

now, and they will find—for self-interest governs all these things, whatever the pride of nations may dictate—it will not divert the course of trade from its easiest channels, and when you have diverted the course of trade through our republic, all that Europe uses of the spices, teas, and silks of the East will come through this channel, here by you, the people of Chicago. [Applause.] I tell you, sir, and I say to this company, you have a right to be proud of what you have done, for you are revolutionizing the commerce of the world. I do not know that any man can now form a judgment of the exceeding importance of this great work; but I am glad, sir, that it has fallen to my lot to support it before the nation, to give my voice and influence in its behalf. [Applause.] I am glad, sir, that it stands recorded there that, through good report and through evil report, I stood by this as I stand by all those great thoroughfares that connect the interests of this great republic with one another. The gentleman alluded to that great international work, the water communication between here and the East, almost as important as the other, and worthy the enterprising people of Chicago to bring before the public, and I trust they will have the intelligence and the power to impress its importance on the whole people of the United States, so that that work shall go hand in hand with the other, and finally be accomplished. [Applause.] Therefore, again I say to you that the importance of this location transcends probably what most men think of it. If you are not to be the first city of this continent, you will never have but two rivals— San Francisco, on the Pacific, may contend the palm of greatness with you, and New York has got to run fast to get out of your way. [Laughter and applause.] You may deem that an extravagant expression, but recollect that New York city had to struggle for one hundred and fifty years before she had the population and wealth that you have to-day. Look at her history, and then at all this you have made up since I visited this, then barren spot, thirty-two years ago, and certainly neither your intelligence nor your enterprise are slow to perceive the great advantages of your location ; and what I have seen to-day convinces me that you will not be slow to appropriate all the advantages you possess. No people of this country have more of intelligence, more of enterprise, more of the American Yankee go-ahead-ativeness than the people of Chicago. [Applause.] I say again, there are but two cities on this continent that can compete with you and your posterity for the palm of greatness.

"And now, as to the excursion. I have said before, and I repeat it here, that it was on the most comprehensive scale of magnificence that I have ever seen. The Company have stopped at nothing that would promote our happiness or bring within our grasp all the intelligence we could possibly acquire on this subject. They stopped at nothing, and there is not a member of that excursion party who would not admit the perfect organization that was brought about by the managers of the excursion. It was thoroughly organized—and, traversing this continent more than fifteen hundred miles, having to use different modes of conveyance, transporting this great company from one point to another without the least confusion or the least delay, was a work that required brains as well as generosity. Their arrangements were all perfect, and the enjoyment of the excursionists was as great as it was possible that it could be made by all that human ingenuity could give, and I believe there is not a man among them but feels to-day, in his heart, gratitude for the opportunities it gave him to be acquainted with our great country. Here I may also say, sir, that we took away out there, among the Pawnees, and brought face to face with barbarism, almost the entire instrumentalities of our highest civilization. We had there a printing-press ; a morning paper was printed in the Platte Valley, beyond the hundreth meridian, and while the Pawnees were dancing their wild dances, the printers were working off a description of the scene. The spectacle was a novel and a gratifying one, and I doubt if, in the history of these times, which amaze and surprise men, there has been anything more surprising than took place on those remote plains. With the printing-press we had the telegraph, that we might in a moment communicate with our friends at home from that distant region among the yells of the aborigines. For one, I enjoyed it more than I can express, and my gratitude to the gentlemen who invited me to participate in this great occasion is greater than I can express. To the people of Chicago, to the Mayor of the city and its officials generally, I also wish to return my most sincere thanks for their abundant hospitalities. They have done all to promote our pleasure, and make interesting this great excursion, that men could do.

" I am thankful that I am enabled to return my thanks thus publicly to all who have contributed to our enjoyment, and with this expression will detain you no longer, as there are to follow me gentlemen who are much better able to describe the scenes through which we have passed. They will now address you."

Senator Wade was followed by Mr. J. C. Dore, the President of the Chicago Board of Trade; Colonel A. W. Johnson, of Maine; Colonel J. H. Howe, Solicitor of the Northwestern Railway; Lord Airlie, of England; Hon. S. S. Hayes, of Chicago; Hon. B. M. Boyer, of Penn.; the Marquis of Chambrun, of France; Hon. J. W. Patterson, U. S. Senator from New Hampshire; General J. H. Simpson, and others, all of whom spoke most enthusiastically of the excursion, and also of the Great West, from which they were now reluctantly returning.

GENERAL SIMPSON'S LETTER FROM NORTH PLATTE.

The following letter, copied from the *Washington Chronicle*, signed " Westward, Ho !" was written by Gen. J. H. Simpson, U. S. Engineers, and President of the Board of Commissioners, appointed by the President of the United States to examine and report, for his acceptance or rejection, completed portions of the Union Pacific Railroad.

The name of General Simpson is also very honorably
identified with some of the most important surveys that
have been made across the continent, by order of the Government, for railroads, wagon roads, and military posts.

It will be found to contain much valuable information
respecting the character and progress of the work; and
it is inserted here by permission of General Simpson, for
the purpose of affording the latest reliable information
upon that subject, as well as a complete and official refu-
tation of the slanderous articles recently published in St.
Louis and other papers, which are evidently hostile to
this road, with reference to the manner in which it has
thus far been constructed:—

NORTH PLATTE STATION, UNION PACIFIC RAILROAD, }
NEBRASKA, *December* 24*th*, 1866.

Editor of the Washington Chronicle :—

I address you from this station on the world's great highway, the
Union Pacific Railroad. The distance from Omaha is two hundred
and ninety-three miles, and it is short of the west end of the completed track twelve miles, making the total number of miles of track in
running condition, west from Omaha, three hundred and five miles.
When we consider that two hundred and sixty miles of this road have
been constructed during the present year in this out-of-the-way country,
to which the iron, rolling stock, pine lumber, and many other essen-
tials of the road had to be transported from St. Louis and St. Joseph
by water, on account of the railroad connection being incomplete over
Iowa, with Chicago, we are struck with amazement and delight at the
boldness, enterprise, and energy with which this great undertaking
has been carried forward by the Company constructing the road.

A road constructed with such celerity naturally conveys the idea
that it has been caused by the level character of the Platte Valley,
through which it runs, and must have been accomplished at the expense of the good character of the track. But one has only to
traverse it, as the writer has done, to assure him that this has not
been the fact.

I know no road in the country, except it may be the great railroads in New York, Pennsylvania, Ohio, and Michigan, which have been perfecting for a score or more of years, that can compare with this read in the general good character of its embankments, cuts, ditches, station houses, water tanks, depots, round houses, machine and car-shops, and all the other adjuncts which are essential to the construction of a first class railroad.

To ride over the road and through the almost limitless valley of the Platte, with a speed equal to that experienced in the great rail-roads of the States I have mentioned, is to start within you ideas of the greatness, power, and progress of our country, which you cannot get in any other way in connection with the arts of peace. The power of the Government was shown in suppressing the late rebellion against the rightful authority of the nation, but equally is it now shown in the peaceful, happy, and yet powerful manner in which it is extending its influence over this whole continent, and ultimately extending the blessings of Christianity and good government over the whole world. Surely we are in the hands of an Infinite and Beneficent Power, who is making this free Government a great instrument for carrying on His gracious purposes with regard to the amelioration of the human race ; and is not all this a blessing for which the whole country should be thankful.

To revert to the already happy effect of this road in shortening distances in time between remote places, the writer received a letter yesterday, the 23d instant, post-marked Washington, December 18th, or five days from the capital of the country ; and this at the forks of the Platte, three hundred miles out on the Plains, and at the close of the wintry month of December. Surely this shows progress towards the Pacific.

All along the road, where the Company has established its stations settlements are springing up rapidly ; and here, at this point whence I write, North Platte Station, *where three weeks ago, there was nothing*, are already some twenty buildings, including a brick engine round-house, calculated for forty engines, founded on a stone foundation, at present nearly completed for ten engines ; a water tank of beautiful proportions, as they all are along the road, kept from freezing by being warmed by a stove, also a fixture in every tank house ; a frame depot of the usual beautiful design ; a large frame hotel, nearly finished, to cost about $18,000 ; a long, spacious, movable building, belonging to

General Casement, and his brother, Daniel Casement, the great track-
layers of the continent, calculated for a store, eating-house, and for
storage purposes; together with sundry other buildings.

To this point the Company think of removing their offices from
Omaha, and establishing it as a more convenient base for furthering
their operations west.   •

The great idea which this Company has in its aims and objects, is
to get this great highway *through* to California; and it is this all-ab-
sorbing purpose which gives unity in all their operations, and has
been the main spring of their hitherto unrivalled success. Already
the route has been definitely fixed to Great Salt Lake, and the prox-
imity to an air line from Chicago, considering the ·difficulties of the
route through the Black Hills, Rocky Mountains proper, and the
Wasatch Range, is a source of heartfelt gratulation.

The Government Commissioners, Generals Simpson, Curtis, and Dr.
White, are now here, examining the last completed section of thirty-
five miles, extending from the two hundred and seventieth to the
three hundred and fifth mile post west from Omaha; and they express
themselves highly pleased with the admirable manner in which the
road has been built throughout. They occupy the beautiful car
which was gotten up by the Quartermaster's Department, during the
ate rebellion, for President Lincoln, and which first carried him when
his mortal remains were borne through a weeping nation, from the
capital of our country to his home at Springfield, Illinois. The Government sold the car to this great national railroad company, and now
it is used by its officers for national purposes in connection with the
progress of this highway of the world.

This main trunk is so admirably linked with the Sioux City branch,
the Mississippi and Missouri Railroad branch, the Hannibal and St.
Joseph Railroad branch, by the way of Atchison, and the Missouri
Pacific branch, west from St. Louis, that all these roads should continue to be fostered by the General Government. These branches give
equal facilities to all parts of our common country, and every citizen,
as well as the Government, should take equal pride in encouraging
lhis greatest of all enterprises.

The writer had nearly forgotten to speak of the railroad connection
with the net of railroads east of Omaha, by the near completion of
the Iowa branch of the Chicago and Northwestern Railroad. This
road the writer rode over last week, from Chicago, as far as St. Johns,

twenty-two miles east of Omaha, and certainly before spring, if not within a month, the connection will be complete all the way from New York to the west end of the Great Pacific Railroad.

Already an Express Company has been organized, called the Western Transportation Company, which is in operation day and night, and transports freight within five days from this, North Platte Station, to Denver. This, again, is progress.

WESTWARD, Ho!

DEATH OF GENERAL CURTIS.

Major-General Samuel R. Curtis, whose name is mentioned in the foregoing letter as one of the Government Commissioners of the Union Pacific Railroad, died very suddenly while returning from this visit to the road. He was riding over from Omaha to Council Bluffs, in a carriage, in company with the other two Commissioners, when he expired almost instantaneously, and was taken to the house of his friend Colonel Nutt, in Council Bluffs, a corpse.

Commissioners, General Simpson and Major White, together with Col. Nutt and Major L. S. Bent, accompanied his remains to his home in Keokuk, where they were received, and escorted to their last resting-place, with distinguished honors.

General Curtis was a civil engineer of great experience and good reputation; an able and distinguished officer in the army during the late rebellion; and an upright, honest man, respected and beloved by all who knew him.

He was one of the earliest advocates and promoters of the Union Pacific Railroad, both in and out of Congress; and lived to see more than three hundred miles of that great work completed, and accepted by the Government.

CONCLUSION.

Since the occurrence of the events hereinbefore recorded, other events have either transpired, or may be
predicted with some degree of certainty, in connection
with the Union Pacific Railroad, to which it may not be
improper to refer, in closing this somewhat prolix and
desultory narrative.

The Directors have fixed the location of the road over
the Black Hill Range of the Rocky Mountains, upon the
route followed by our party a portion of the distance on
its return trip from the Laramie Plains.

After three years spent in making the most careful
surveys of the Rocky Mountain Passes, extending from
the sources of the South Plate, on the south, to Fort
Laramie on the north, it was found that this route would
be much more direct; and could be built in less time,
and with much lower maximum grades than any of the
other routes surveyed.

The route as located, leaves the valley of the South
Platte, at the mouth of Lodge Pole Creek, opposite
Julesburgh, and follows up the valley of that creek
about one hundred miles, when it crosses obliquely the
divide between Lodge-Pole, and Crow Creeks. And
thence across Crow Creek to the divide between that
stream and Lone-Tree Creek, which divide it follows to
the summit of the Black Hill Range at Evans' Pass.
From the summit it follows down the southwesterly
slope of the Black Hills to the Laramie Plains.

Beyond this nothing has been decided upon with reference to the location, although several routes have been
surveyed to the eastern line of California.

This location leaves Denver city about one hundred
miles to the south of the main through line of the Union

Pacific Railroad; but a branch road, over a very good route, may, and probably will be constructed from Denver and the rich mineral regions of that portion of Colorado, to the main line, within one or two years.

The route through Denver and Berthoud Pass was found to be comparatively impracticable—and the Company could not consistently bend the line nearer Denver, without discriminating too much against the through business of the road.

The staging from the end of the track to Denver is now reduced to from thirty-six to forty hours; and a fast freight line has been established for the transportation of freight, from the end of the track to any point in the western Territories.

The track laying was suspended in December, at a point three hundred and five miles west of Omaha, on account of cold weather, and the want of materials. The grading is completed about fifty miles, and the ties are provided for more than one hundred miles west of that point. A sufficient quantity of iron rails has been purchased to extend the track to the Laramie river, a distance of two hundred and seventy-one miles from the end of the present track; and if an excursion party should start for the end of the track, just one year from the time that the late excursion party left New York, it will be quite sure to make its last camping ground as far west as the Laramie Plains.

The *Great connecting link* has been completed from Chicago to the Missouri River opposite Omaha; and preparations are now being made to construct a bridge over the Missouri during the coming season; when this is done, and the track of the Union Pacific Railroad is extended to the Laramie Plains, the traveller may ride in the same car from New York city, a distance of nineteen hundred and sixty-seven miles, on his way westward across the Continent—and he must not be surprised if, during the year 1869, he can continue in the same car to Great Salt Lake City, a distance of two thousand four hundred and twenty-eight miles from New York.

So mote it be.